UNWIN...TIONS

FU...NES

**INCLUDING
FOLLOW ON
ACTIVITIES**

EDITED BY TREVOR MILLUM

Unwin Hyman English Series

Series editor: Roy Blatchford
Advisers: Jane Leggett and Gervase Phinn

Unwin Hyman Short Stories
Openings   edited by Roy Blatchford
Round Two   edited by Roy Blatchford
School's OK   edited by Josie Karavasil and Roy Blatchford
Stepping Out   edited by Jane Leggett
That'll Be The Day   edited by Roy Blatchford
Sweet and Sour   edited by Gervase Phinn
It's Now or Never   edited by Jane Leggett and Roy Blatchford
Pigs is Pigs   edited by Trevor Millum
Dreams and Resolutions   edited by Roy Blatchford
Snakes and Ladders   edited by Hamish Robertson
Crying For Happiness   edited by Jane Leggett
Crime Busters   edited by Brian Pateman and Jennie Sidney
Shorties   edited by Roy Blatchford
First Class   edited by Michael Bennett

Unwin Hyman Collections
Free As I Know   edited by Beverley Naidoo
In Our Image   edited by Andrew Goodwyn
Solid Ground   edited by Jane Leggett and Sue Libovitch
Northern Lights   edited by Leslie Wheeler and Douglas Young

Unwin Hyman Plays
Stage Write   edited by Gervase Phinn
Scriptz   edited by Ian Lumsden
Right On Cue   edited by Gervase Phinn

Published in 1989 by
Unwin Hyman Limited
15/17 Broadwick Street
London W1V 1FP

Selection and notes © Trevor Millum 1989
The copyright of each story and poem remains the property of the author.

British Library Cataloguing in Publication Data

Funnybones
1 English literature, 1945—
Anthologies
820.8'00914

ISBN 0-04-440297-X

Typeset in Great Britain by TJB Photosetting Ltd., Grantham, Lincolnshire
Printed in Great Britain by Billing & Sons Ltd., Worcester
Series cover design by Iain Lanyon
Cover illustration by Terry McKenna

CONTENTS

Introduction by Trevor Millum   v

'Bone Lines'   Trevor Millum   1

January 1943 – At Sea (from *Adolf Hitler –
My Part in His Downfall*)   Spike Milligan   3

Unreliable Memoirs   Clive James   10

The Loaded Dog   Henry Lawson   21

Poems – Group A:

   'Daily Dilemmas'   Natasha Josefowitz   29

   'The Diet'   Maureen Burge   30

   'E322 – or Is My Mother Trying to Kill Me?'
   Trevor Millum   31

   'Giving Up Smoking'   Wendy Cope   33

Goat's Tobacco (from *Boy*)   Roald Dahl   34

Where Did our Pete Find this Tiger? (from *Private – Keep Out!*)
Gwen Grant   38

Snake in the Grass   Helen Cresswell   47

A Night on the Mountain (from *The Education of Little Tree*)
Forrest Carter   54

Poems – Group B:

   'Our Solar System'   Eric Finney   66

   'Dead Thick'   Brian Patten   69

   'An Essay Justifying the Place of Science in the School
   Curriculum'   Jayne Hollinson   70

Thoughts on Paper   (from *Bitter-Sweet Dreams*)
Maria Morris   72

Southward Bound (from *Scully*)   Alan Bleasdale   78

Abscess Makes the Heart Grow Fonder (from *How Was It For
You?*)   Maureen Lipman   96

Poems – Group C:

    'nobody loses all the time'   e e cummings   99

    'The Grange'   Stevie Smith   101

    'Poor but Honest'   Anon.   103

    'Exploding Heads'   Trevor Millum   105

House-hunting (from *Love Forty*)   Sue Limb   107

At Longitude and Latitude   J.P. Donleavy   115

Dear Mary (from *Letters from a Faint-Hearted Feminist*)
   Jill Tweedie   117

'Please Keep Off The Grass'   Peter Tinsley   120

Fiddler On The Roof   Alan Coren   121

Follow On (Prose)   126

Extended Assignments   144

Follow On (Poems)   146

Further Reading   151

Acknowledgements   153

Introduction

Many a comedian has declared that humour is a serious business. Everyone knows there's nothing worse than a joke which falls flat, and writing which sets out to be funny sets itself a difficult task. Calling a book Funnybones sets up expectations which are hard to meet. Better perhaps to come across a story which amuses you without knowing beforehand it is meant to be funny!

If the writer of humorous stories or poems is a risk-taker, I too have taken a risk in compiling a collection of pieces of writing which I (together with friends and pupils with varying tastes) think are funny. It's a risk worth taking for a number of reasons. One is to introduce a cross-section of writers to an audience who may only have heard of one or two of them. It makes a change from all the very earnest pieces in many anthologies. Perhaps more importantly, I think it is crucial to show that we value humour and recognize its importance as a major component of our humanity. It is also an opportunity to investigate the way in which we deal with problems and anxieties by invoking laughter. And, of course, humour is one of the most effective ways of making a serious point.

I would say this to prospective readers: Don't expect to find each piece hilarious. Publishers in their blurbs frequently claim that their books are 'hilarious' or 'riotous' and the reader is usually disappointed. It's a rare piece of writing which makes you laugh out loud. Three or four of the items in this book had that effect on me, but I won't tell you which ones. Others made me smile, or laugh inwardly. There are many types of humorous writing and many different senses of humour. If you find some writing in this collection which appeals to your sense of humour, I'll be pleased. If you find a lot, I'll be delighted. If you don't find any—perhaps the problem lies with you!

This selection is deliberately broad. At one end of the scale, 'Goat's Tobacco', from *Boy* is written for younger children but I have heard parts of it read to an adult audience who thoroughly enjoyed it. At the other end of the scale, Clive James writes for a definitely mature readership but I have read extracts of his writing to young people who were obviously very amused. Along another spectrum, the extract from *The Education of Little Tree* is gently amusing in its irony (with an injection of farce towards the end) while Spike Milligan is comic throughout.

The collection, then, is addressed to older secondary pupils, seeing them very much as young adults rather than older children.

Some pieces will appeal to younger children as well and most will appeal to adults. (The more we have experienced, the more there is to laugh at—and that often means laughing at ourselves.) But whatever the age of the audience, these stories, even more than most, benefit from being read aloud because there is nothing like laughter for triggering more laughter.

In the 'Follow On' section I have tried to vary the activities so that there is always something suitable for less able or less motivated pupils as well as more demanding items. Many of the suggestions require or lend themselves to a variety of oral work. They also offer a range of approaches which can be adopted with other texts. Some could lead to GCSE coursework assignments and standard grade folio work or help in the preparation of examination essays. I have tried to tread the difficult path between treating humour too ponderously and giving the impression that humour cannot be taken seriously.

The 'Follow On' activities are divided under three broad headings: Before, During and After Reading. The prose 'Follow On' comes first, then the poetry 'Follow On' which looks at the three groups of poems in turn. The intention is that the students should engage with the texts as closely as possible, from predicting storylines to analysing motivations. Teachers using the collection are therefore recommended to preview the 'Follow On' section before reading the stories, poems and extracts with students.

Trevor Millum

Bone Lines

Have you ever − − − − − − − − − −?
Where's your lumbar vertebrae?
Do you know where the nearest − − − − −?
How's your clavicle today?

Have you heard − − − − − − − − − − − −?
Note the − − − − − − way he talks.
No good saying it's a − − − − − −
That's just the way he walks.

Cram these in your crowded cranium:
Scapula, sacrum, xiphisternum.
Weren't they on the − − − − − tongue?
Then this is one good way to learn 'em.

Shake hands with your − − − − − − − − − − −,
Use your femurs on the run
And when your skeleton is weary,
Sit down on your − − − − − − −!

(*See next page for answers.*)

Bone Lines

Have you ever met a tarsal?
Where's your lumbar vertebrae?
Do you know where the nearest pub is?
How's your clavicle today?

Have you heard Pat tella story?
Note the humerus way he talks.
No good saying it's fibula,
That's just the way he walks.

Cram these in your crowded cranium:
Scapula, sacrum, xiphisternum.
Weren't they on the tibia tongue?
Then this is one good way to learn 'em.

Shake hands with your meta car pals,
Use your femurs on the run
And when your skeleton is weary,
Sit down on your ischium!

Trevor Millum

J anuary 1943—At Sea

*The writer's regiment has been posted overseas and the troop
ship has just left Liverpool.*

By dawn the regiment were at sea (but then we always had
been). Reveille was at 07:00. Sailors wore bells to tell the time.
They would shake their wrists, shout 'Six bells', swallow cups
of hot tar, sing several 'Yo Ho Ho's', tie knots in each other's
appendages and hornpipe the dawn away. Breakfast was at
eight o'clock bells. Two men from each table were detailed to
collect it from the galley.

Joke of the day.

'Captain, I've brought your breakfast up.'

'Serves you right for eating it.'

After a breakfast of kippers, anchors, and scurvy, we had
roll-call. There had been soul-searching at high level as we
were unexpectedly excused boots and allowed plimsolls, at
night we were excused plimsolls and allowed feet. The con-
fined air-tight sleeping of 10,000 hairy gunners below-decks
had filled the air with a reek of stale cigarettes, sweat, and a
taste in the mouth like the inside of a long distance runner's
sock. We groped our way through the fog on to the main deck.
The day was dove-grey, low cloud, a slight green-grey swell.
We gulped in the clean air. During the night several ships had
joined the convoy. Two low-slung destroyers were the out-
riders. Alongside floated serene, silent white seagulls, whose
dignity dissolved into shrieking scavengerism at the sight of
ship's offal. There was a canteen on the main deck, open from
ten till twelve, then three to six, then eight till ten, for the sale
of tea, and biscuits that tasted like the off-cuts of hardboard.
Harry and I promenaded the decks. From what we could
glean, the *Otranto* was a fine ship: perhaps it was, but why did
the captain sleep in a lifeboat? Harry and I promenaded the
decks. At nine o'clock and a half bells, we heard BBC news

over the ship's speakers. The Russians were advancing on all fronts. Where *did* they get the money? Gunner Simms, an amateur astronomer with a compass from a Christmas cracker, had worked out we were going south. Harry and I promenaded the decks knowing full well we were going south. The rest of the day was spent doing nothing except going south. In our wake the sea was a mixture of bubbling turquoise and white. The seagulls stayed with us two days and nights, then suddenly left. Every third day we were to wear boots to stop our feet getting soft. Whereas the days were getting warmer, the weather was deteriorating. (The worst of travelling on the cheap.) The *Otranto*, with capacity loading, was low in the water. She started to do a figure-of-eight roll. The first seasickness started. In the three days since leaving, the convoy got bigger by six ships and two destroyers; these always joined us after dark. Still no news where we were going. Gunner Simms thought we were on the fringe of Biscay. I'd suffered the Bay many times. I knew how bad it could get and get it did. On the night of January 13th, already in heavy seas, we hit a force nine gale. Christ. Seas became mountainous. We listed alarmingly. Furniture broke loose. Crockery shattered on decks. A sliding table broke Sergeant Hendricks's legs. So he was out of it, though, of course, he could fight lying down. Ha! Ha! Seeing a man upright was a thing of the past. I went round saying 'What's your angle, man?' At night the hammocks swung like violent pendulums. The top of Gunner Jack Shapiro's came undone. His lovely head hit the floor. He lay there. Was he asleep? Or unconscious *and* asleep? To bring him round we would have to wait till he woke up and became unconscious. With true military gallantry we left him there. On Captain's orders, we all slept in life-jackets. Bloody uncomfortable. You realized what a woman with a forty-two inch bosom felt like sleeping face downwards on her back. (Pardon?).

That night, the storm raging, I fell into a not-too-peaceful sleep. Next day. Oh dear. Men sick everywhere; some managed to get to the toilets, but as the days passed and they weakened they were sick where they stood. I was all right, but I kept having to leap clear. It was my turn to collect breakfast. With two heavy containers I swayed like Blondin over the

Niagara. To complicate matters, it was another boot day. Decks were soaking wet. Containers full, I left the galley. The ship tilted. I started to slide at increasing speed towards the red-hot stoves. 'Quick,' I yelled. 'Phone Lloyds of London and insure me against catching fire at sea whilst carrying porridge!' A hairy cook grabbed me just in time. 'This could mean promotion for you,' I told him. There was food for twelve, but only two takers: Edgington and me. We enjoyed liberal portions of sausages, bacon, bread and butter, tea, jam. Then started all over again. All to the sound of great agonized retching groans. Feeling fine, we tried to bring joy to our less fortunate comrades by saying 'Cold greasy tripe and raw eggs!' We had to be quick. Edgington and I promenaded the decks. Harry stopped: 'If only I had a tube.'

'Why?'

'It's quicker by tube.'

With eighty per cent illness we had to take turns on the antiaircraft guns. The night I was on was a frightening affair. One of the men on Bofor guns forward was washed overboard. Next morning, there was a service in the canteen for him. Poor bastard. The storm never let up. It was only this that prevented U-boat attacks, though I know many a sick-covered wreck who would rather have had calm seas and been torpedoed. A poor green-faced thing asked, 'Isn't there *any* bloody cure for seasickness?'

'Yes,' I said. 'Sit under a tree.' I had to be quick.

Gunner Olins had been told deaf people never get sick. He spent the rest of the storm with his fingers in his ears. The ship, now, was one big vomit bucket. On the night of the 14th we had passed through the Straits of Gibraltar into the Mediterranean and gone was the gale all was calm. The Med???? This threw the speculation book wide open. Bombardier Rossi was taking bets. Malta 6–4, India 20–1, Libya 6–4 on, Algeria 11–10 on, Bournemouth 100–1. Most of us thought it would be Algeria. As we passed further through the Straits, the sea went calm like a satisfied mistress. Darkness gathered quickly, and lo! across the straits were the glittering lights of all-electric Tangiers! The port rail was crowded. We hadn't seen so many lights since they went out that September in 1939. I thought sadly of blacked-out Britain, but look at the money we were saving! With Doug Kidgell I watched the magic glow of Tangiers.

'Think you could swim to it?'

'Yesss,' he said. 'It's only about three to five miles.' He was a superb swimmer and, for that matter, so was I – (100 metres Champion, Convent of Jesus and Mary, Poona. I could swim any nun off her feet). I told him if we did we'd be sure of ending the war alive. 'They'd make us,' said Doug, 'do time in the nick.' 'That's right, we'd be saved in the nick of time.' We didn't swim to Tangiers that night. Tannoys came to life. 'Cigarettes out on deck.' It was dark. Harry and I promenaded the decks. The night was warm, clear, starry. The air was like balm. Phosphorus trailed in our wake like undersea glow-worms. We were given permission to sleep up on the top deck, provided no late-night customs were performed at ship's rails. The joy of lying on your back facing a starry sky is something I remember for its sheer simplicity. Not that we weren't living a simple life. Oh no, we were all bloody simple or we wouldn't be in this boat. With the storm behind us, Chaterjack, MC, DSO, tired of throwing empty whisky bottles overboard, decided life was dull. The band was to play for dancing in the Officers' Lounge from 21:30 bells to 23:59. Regarding this, I quote from a letter I had from Chaterjack in March, 1958, in which he recalls the occasion – 'Many episodes may well come up during your reminiscences on Friday [the day of the D Battery reunion]. One vivid one to me starts as early as our embarkation at Liverpool: we had been well warned by RHQ that if we were spotted trying to camouflage the band instruments amongst the embarkation stores, they would go into the sea. Being fairly efficient soldiers, we embarked the band—camouflaged as I know not what—and there the matter ended for the moment. It ended until we had survived the Bay of Biscay through which the vessel rolled almost over the danger angle, though most people were below decks, beyond caring, slung in hammocks and racked with seasickness. Surviving all this, we turned towards Gib., the sun shone, the sea was calm and a band was badly wanted. RHQ asked shamefacedly if we had wangled it on board, we admitted, poker-faced, that we had—all was well, the band played, people struggled on deck, the sun shone and we approached Algiers in full fine fettle.'

It was fun rummaging in the hold among Bren carriers and cannons to find a drum kit. 'Oh God,' said Alf, 'my guitar's all packed up for the trip.' 'Well,' I said, 'let's unpack it, we can pretend it's Christmas.' He hit me. That night we were in great form. It's a great feeling playing Jazz. Most certainly it never started a war. The floor space was limited, and crowded with pump-handle couples. There were service ladies, with a pre-dominance of Queen Alexandra Nursing Sisters—(where were *they* when the decks were strewn with seasick soldiers?). We saw strange gyrations as the ship rolled the dancers into a corner, then rolled them across to the other one. To include 'Cocking of the Legs' we played a reel. Sure enough, they responded like Pavlov's dogs. At the evening's end Major Chaterjack, MC, DSO, thanked the band and passed the hat round for some financial tribute. Mean bastards. We'd have got more it we'd sold the hat. We had to restrain Harry from playing the Warsaw Concerto. Major Chaterjack, MC, DSO, made it up by giving us half a bottle of whisky. Swinging gently in hammocks, we passed the bottle back and forth until we fell into a smiling sleep. It was the best day we'd had at sea. From now on the weather improved. Those who had suffered sickness were now strong enough to lie down without help. The morning after the dance was perfect. Clear sky. No wind. Calm sea. We were dive-bombed. 'Tin hats on,' boomed the Tannoy. Gun crews were all caught with their pants down. (There was some kind of medical inspection at the time.) Chaterjack's batman awakened him: 'Sir, an Iti plane is bombing us.' 'Don't worry,' said Chaterjack, 'he's allowed to,' and added, 'Did you get his number?' It was an old lumbering three-engined Caproni. We let fly a few rounds at him, it didn't seem fair, like shooting a grandmother. So we just waved him goodbye. After this attack, gun crews became trigger-happy. The sight of a seagull was the signal for thunderous barrages. It had to be stopped. The ship's Captain addressed us over the Tannoy. 'Gentlemen, all seagulls in the area are unarmed, can we refrain from shooting at them? Thank you.' Edgington had something to say about this. 'Seagulls yes, but what about fish?' We were travelling through fish-infested waters, many of them sympathetic to the German cause. 'You're right, Colonel,' I said. 'There should be regular fish-inspections, each being tasted for identification.'

Me: 'Sir, this fish tastes like a Gestapo Sergeant.'

Edgington: 'Right, drown it, at once.'

Me: 'It's not frightened of water.'

Edgington: 'Then drown it on land. Poison a hill and make him eat it.'

Me: 'Yes.'

Edgington: 'That "yes" sounds very suspicious.'

Me: 'Don't worry, it's one of ours.'

Edgington: 'Good, you can stand by me to rely on you.'

Me: 'I shall always remember you like that.' (Here I point to a coil of greasy rope.)

Edgington: 'Ah, I was very poor then but now...'

Me: 'But now what?'

Edgington: 'But now I was very poor then.'

We were only twenty-one.

The end of the voyage was nigh. We wanted to get ashore before the equipment was out of date. Over the Tannoy: 'Good morning. Colonel Meadows speaking. I'm going to put you all out of your agony.' (He was too late for me.) I can now tell you our destination.'(CHEERS) 'We are to land at Algiers, as reinforcements for the 1st Army; we will be fighting alongside the Americans, who will be welcomed into this theatre of operations.' 'So, we're going to an operating theatre,'grinned Harry. 'We should be docking at 10.30 a.m. tomorrow. From there we will go to a Transit Camp for brief training. We should be in action three weeks from now'. (Mixed groans and cheers.) 'Good luck to you all.' Cries of 'Good Luck Mate'. Algiers? Wasn't that where Charles Boyer once had it off with Hedy Lamar in the Kasbah? Mind you, they got out while the going was good. The rest of the day was spent packing kit. We were issued with an air-mail letter, in which we were allowed to say we'd arrived safe and sound. News which would now make everybody at home happy. From now, all mail was censored. We were no longer allowed to give the number of troops, measurements of guns and ammo returns to the German Embassy in Spain. This, of course, would cut our income down considerably. So there it was, tomorrow North Africa. I wrote the name on a bit of paper, it would come in useful. That evening with the sun setting, we all gathered around Major Chaterjack on the promenade deck and sang old songs. The sea was still, ships were at slow speed, as the sounds of 'You are my sunshine', 'Run Rabbit Run' and 'Drink to me only' were wafted across the waters. It all seemed very nostalgic. It must have struck terror into the breasts of any listening Germans.

CLIVE JAMES

Unreliable Memoirs

These two extracts are taken from the Australian writer and broadcaster's
autobiography Unreliable Memoirs.

I

I was coping with physics and chemistry well enough while
Mr Ryan was still teaching them. But Mr Ryan was due for
retirement, an event which was hastened by an accident in the
laboratory. He was showing us how careful you had to be
when handling potassium in the presence of water. Certainly
you had to be more careful than he was. The school's entire
supply of potassium ignited at once. Wreathed by dense
smoke and lit by garish flames, the stunned Mr Ryan looked
like a superannuated Greek god in receipt of bad news. The
smoke enveloped us all. Windows being thrown open, it
jetted into what passed for a playground, where it hung
around like some sinister leftover from a battle on the Somme.
Shocked, scorched and gassed, Mr Ryan was carried away,
never to return.

Back from his third retirement came Mary Luke. A chronic
shortage of teachers led to Mary Luke being magically resur-
rected after each burial. Why he should have been called Mary
was a datum lost in antiquity. The school presented him with
a pocket watch every time he retired. Perhaps that was a mistake. It might have been the massed ticking that kept him
alive. Anyway, Mary Luke, having already ruined science for
a whole generation of schoolboys, came back from the
shadows to ruin science for me.

Mary was keen but incomprehensible. The first thing he
said at the start of every lesson, whether of physics or chemistry,
was, 'Make a Bunsen burner.' He was apparently convinced
that given the right encouragement we would continue our
science studies in makeshift laboratories at home. So we

might have done, if we could have understood anything else he said. Unfortunately 'Make a Bunsen burner' was his one remaining fathomable sentence. In all other respects his elocution made my late grandfather sound like Leslie Howard. The same comparison applied to his physical appearance. How could anyone be that old without being dead? But there were definite signs of life. The mouth moved constantly. 'Combustioff off magnesioff,' Mary would announce keenly. 'Magnesioff off ixidoff off hydrogoff off givoff off.' Worriedly I slid the cap off the inverted jar and ignited the gaseous contents to prove that hydrogoff had been givoff off. Carefully I drew the apparatus in my book, already aware that these preliminary experiments would be the last I would ever understand.

Perhaps I was never cut out for chemistry. But I had a right to think that physics might have lain within my scope. I impressed Mary with my precocious knowledge of the planets, which I could name in their order outwards from the sun. Mary looked momentarily blank at the mention of Pluto, but otherwise he seemed well pleased. A novel rearrangement of his lips took place which I guessed to be a smile. The teeth thereby revealed featured eye-catching areas of green amongst the standard amber and ochre. If only we could have stuck to astronomy. Instead, Mary sprang optics on us. 'Thoff angloff off incidoff,' he informed us, 'equoff thoff angloff off reflectioff.' We fiddled dutifully with pins and mirrors. I had the sinking feeling of being unable to understand. The moment of breakdown came when Mary started exploring the different properties of concave and convex mirrors. I couldn't see which was which when he held them up. More importantly, I couldn't tell the difference when he said their names. 'Thoff miroff off concoff,' he explained carefully, 'off thoff miroff off convoff.' Proud of having made things clear, he smiled fixedly, giving us a long look at his wrecked teeth. What was going *on* in that mouth of his? I could see things moving.

But some of the other boys seemed to understand Mary even if I couldn't, and anyway in the straight mathematical subjects I had no excuse. The teaching might have been uninspired but it was sound enough. Besides, if I had had any mathematical talent I probably wouldn't even have needed teaching. As things were, I remained good at mathematics as long as mathematics remained arithmetic and algebra. I was passable at trigonometry. But when calculus came in, the lights went out. My average marks gradually started to shelve downwards. Things weren't helped by the weekly classes in woodwork and metalwork. I could handle technical drawing well enough, helped by my skill at lettering, but when I entered the workshop I was a gone goose. Metalwork was bad: anything I put in the lathe refused to come out true. It would start off as a cylinder and end up as a blob. So much for my dream of building new jet engines to outclass the Rolls-Royce Avon and the Armstrong Siddeley Sapphire, of designing aircraft whose power and beauty would enrol them among the masterpieces of Sydney Camm, Kurt Tank and Willy Messerschmitt. Woodwork was even worse. Nobody whose hands are not naturally dry can ever be a good carpenter, and I suffered badly from sweaty hands. My hands started to sweat with fear from the moment I put on my calico apron. By the time the woodwork teacher had finished explaining what we had to do my hands would be dripping like taps. Wet hands leave a film on wood that renders it hard to plane. Our first job was to make a breadboard. The breadboard had to be made from half a dozen lengths of wood glued together edge to edge. For this to succeed the edges had to be planed true. I kept on and on from week to week, planing away at my half dozen pieces. It took me an entire term of classes before I got them true. By that time they were like chopsticks. When I glued my breadboard together it was the right length but only two inches wide. You couldn't have cut a French loaf on it.

II
Basic Training

National Service was designed to turn boys into men and make the Yellow Peril think twice about moving south. It was universally known as Nasho – a typically Australian diminutive. Once you were in it, four years went by before you were out of it: there was a three-week camp every year, plus numerous parades. But the most brutal fact about Nasho was the initial 77-day period of basic training, most of which took place at Ingleburn. Each new intake of gormless youth was delivered into the hands of regular army instructors who knew everything about licking unpromising material into shape. When we stepped off the bus at Ingleburn, they were already screaming at us. Screaming sergeants and corporals appeared suddenly out of huts. I stood clutching my Globite suitcase and wondered what had gone wrong with my life. While I goggled at a screaming sergeant, I was abruptly blown sideways by a bellow originating from somewhere behind my right ear. Recovering, I turned to face Ronnie the One.

His real name was Warrant Officer First Class Ronald McDonald, but he was known throughout the army as Ronnie the One. Responsible for battalion discipline, he had powers of life and death over all non-commissioned personnel and could even bring charges against officers up to the rank of captain. His appearance was almost inconceivably unpleasant. A pig born looking like him would have demanded plastic surgery. His brass gleamed like gold and his leather like mahogany, but the effect was undone by his khaki drills, which despite being ironed glass smooth were perpetually soaked with sweat. Ronnie the One dripped sweat even on a cold day. It was not just because he was fat, although he had a behind like an old sofa. It was because he was always screaming so hard. At that moment he was screaming directly at me. 'GEDYAHAYAHCARD!' Later on a translator told me that this meant 'Get your hair cut' and could generally be taken as a friendly greeting, especially if you could still see his eyes. When Ronnie was really annoyed his face swelled up and turned purple like the rear end of an amorous baboon.

For the next eleven weeks I was running flat out, but no matter how fast my feet moved, my mind was moving even faster. It was instantly plain to me that only cunning could ensure survival. Among the university students in our intake, Wokka Clark was undoubtedly the golden boy. Already amateur middleweight champion of NSW, he was gorgeous to behold. But he couldn't take the bullshit. What happened to him was like a chapter out of *From Here to Eternity*. They applauded him in the boxing ring at night and screamed at him all day. That summer the noon temperature was a hundred plus. Ronnie the One would take Wokka out on the parade ground and drill him till he dropped. The reason Wokka dropped before Ronnie did was simple. All Ronnie had on his head was a cap. Wokka had on a steel helmet. The pack on his back was full of bricks. After a few weeks of that, plus guard duty every night that he wasn't boxing, even Wokka was obeying orders.

You couldn't fight them. Even the conscientious objectors ended up looking after the regimental mascot—a bulldog called Onslow who looked like Ronnie's handsome younger brother. It was like one of Kenny Mears's games of marbles: nobody was allowed not to play. I could appreciate the psychology of it. The first task when training new recruits is to disabuse them of the notion that life is fair. Otherwise they will stand rooted to the spot when they first come up against people who are trying to kill them. But my abstract understanding of what was going on impinged only tangentially on the concrete problem of getting through the day without landing myself in the kind of trouble that would make the next day even more impossibly difficult than it was going to be anyway.

Something about my general appearance annoyed Ronnie. There were a thousand trainees in the intake but I was among the select handful of those whose aspect he couldn't abide. I could be standing in a mess queue, Ronnie would be a dot in the distance, and suddenly his voice would arrive like incoming artillery. 'GEDDABIGGAHAD!' He meant that I should get a bigger hat. He didn't like the way it sat on top of my head. Perhaps he just didn't like my head, and wanted the whole thing covered up. The drill that I had learned in Boys' Brigade saved my life. When it came to square-bashing, it turned out that the years I had spent interpreting Captain Andrews's commands had given me a useful insight into what Ronnie was likely to mean by his shouts and screams. When Ronnie yelled 'ABARD HARGH!' I knew almost straight away that it must mean 'about turn'. Thus I was able to turn decisively with the many, instead of dithering with the few.

On the parade ground Peebles drew most of the lightning. So unco-ordinated that he was to all intents and purposes a spastic, Peebles should not have been passed medically fit. But since he had been, the Army was stuck with him. After a month of training, when Ronnie shouted 'ABARD HARGH!' 999 soldiers would smartly present their backs and Peebles would be writhing on the ground, strangled by the sling of his rifle. For Peebles the day of reckoning came when he obeyed an order to fix bayonets. This was one of Ronnie's most frightening orders. It had the verb at the end, as in German or Latin. In English the order would have sounded something like: 'Bayonets...fix!' Bellowed by Ronnie, it came out as: BAHAYONED...FEE!' The last word was delivered as a high-pitched, almost supersonic, scream. It was succeeded on this occasion by another scream, since Peebles's bayonet, instead of appearing at the end of his rifle, was to be seen protruding from the back of the soldier standing in front of him. After that, they used to mark Peebles present at company parade every morning but lose him behind a tree on the way to battalion parade, where he was marked absent.

My kit, not my drill, was what got me into trouble. For once in my life I had to make my own bed every morning, without fail, and lay out for inspection my neatly polished and folded belongings. Since the penalty for not doing this properly was to have the whole lot thrown on the floor and be obliged to start again, I gradually got better at it, but I never became brilliant. National Servicemen had to wax and polish their webbing instead of just powdering it with blanco. It was a long process which bored me, and the same fingers which had been so tacky at woodwork were still likely to gum up the job. The problem became acute when it was my platoon's turn to mount guard. Throughout the entire twenty-four hours it was on duty, the guard was inspected, supervised, harassed and haunted by Ronnie the One. The initial inspection of kit, dress and rifle lasted a full hour. Ronnie snorted at my brass, retched at my webbing, and turned puce when he looked down the barrel of my rifle. 'THASSNODDAGHARDRIVAL!' he yelled. He meant that it was not a guard rifle. 'ISSFUL-LAPADAYDAHS!' He meant that it was full of potatoes. I looked down the barrel. I had spent half a day pulling it through until it glowed like El Dorado's gullet. Now I saw that a single speck of grit had crept into it.

In the guard-house we had to scrub the floors and tables, whitewash the walls and polish the undersides of the drawing pins on the notice board. When we went out on picket we could not afford to relax for a moment, since Ronnie could be somewhere in the vi-cinity preparing to do his famous Banzai charge. At two o'clock in the morning I was guarding the trans-port park. It was raining. Sitting down in the sentry box, I had the brim of my hat unbuttoned and was hanging from the collar of my groundsheet, praying for death. I had my rifle inside my ground sheet with me, so that I could fold my hands on its muzzle, lean my chin on the cushion formed by my hands under the cape and gently nod off while still looking reasonably alert. I had calculated that Ronnie would not come out in the rain. This proved to be a bad guess. I thought the sentry box had been struck by lightning, but it was merely Ronnie's face going off like a purple grenade about a foot in front of mine. I came to attention as if electrocuted and tried to shoulder arms. Since the rifle was still inside my groundsheet, merely to attempt this manoeuvre was bound to yield Peebles-like results. Ronnie informed me, in a tirade which sounded and felt like an atomic attack, that he had never seen anything like it in his life.

The inevitable consequence was extra kitchen duty. I can safely say that I did more of this than anybody else in the bat-talion. While everybody else was out in the donga learning to disguise themselves as ant-hills and sneak up on the enemy, I was in the kitchen heading a crack team of cleaners composed of no-hopers like Peebles. The kitchen was as big as an aircraft hangar. All the utensils were on an enormous scale. The smallest dixies would be four feet long, two feet across and three feet deep. Lined with congealed custard and rhubarb, they took half an hour each to clean. The biggest dixie was the size of a Bessemer converter and mounted on gimbals. I was lowered into it on a rope. When I hit the bottom it rang like a temple gong. After the kitchen sergeant was satisfied that the dixie was shining like silver he pulled a crank and I was tipped out, smothered in mashed potato.

It must have been while I was inside the dixie that I missed out on the chance to volunteer for Infantry. That was how I found myself in the Assault Pioneers—the one specialist course that nobody sane wanted to be on, since it involved land mines, booby traps and detonators. In the long run the lethality of the subject proved to be a boon. National Service was winding to an end by that stage—ours was to be the last intake—and the government didn't want any mother's son getting killed at the eleventh hour. So instead of burying mines for us to dig up, they buried rocks. While our backs were turned, they would bury a hundred rocks in a careful pattern. We would move through the area, probing the earth with our bayonets, and dig up two hundred. It wasn't as glamorous as being in, say, the mortar platoon, but I came to appreciate the lack of excitement, especially after we were all marched out to the range and given a demonstration of what the mortar specialists had learned.

The mortars in question were the full three inches across the barrel—not the two-inch pipes that had little more than nuisance value, but really effective weapons which could throw a bomb over a mountain and kill everything within a wide radius at the point of impact. A thousand of us, including the colonel and all his officers, sat around the rim of a natural amphitheatre while the mortar teams fired their weapons. All looked downwards at the mortars with fascination, except for Ronnie the One, who was down with the mortars looking upwards, tirelessly searching for anyone with too small a hat. Team after team loaded and fired. The bomb was dropped into the mortar and immediately departed towards the stratosphere, where it could be heard—and even, momentarily, seen—before it dived towards its target, which was a large cross on a nearby hill. You saw the blast, then you heard the sound. It was a bit like watching Ronnie having a heart attack on the horizon.

Every team did its job perfectly until the last. The last team was Wokka Clark and Peebles. They had to do *something* with Peebles. If they had put him in the Pioneers he probably would have bitten the detonator instead of the fuse. It went without saying that he could not be allowed to drive a truck or fire a Vickers machine gun, especially after the way he had distinguished himself on the day everyone in the battalion had had to throw a grenade. (One at a time we entered the throwing pit. The sergeant handed you a grenade, from which you removed the pin. You then threw the grenade. When he handed Peebles a grenade, Peebles removed the pin and handed the grenade back to him.) The safest thing to do with Peebles was team him up with Wokka, who was so strong that he could throw the base plate of a three-inch mortar twenty yards. All Peebles had to do was wait until Wokka had done the calibrations and then drop in the bomb. He must have done it successfully scores of times in practice. He did it quite smoothly this time too, except that the bomb went in upside down.

If you were to rig a vacuum cleaner to blow instead of suck and then point it at a pile of dust, you would get some idea of what those thousand supposedly disciplined men did a split second after they noticed the bomb going into the mortar with its fins sticking up instead of down. They just melted away. Some tried to dig themselves into the earth. Some started climbing trees. But most of us ran. I was running flat out when an officer went past me at head height, flapping his arms like a swan. Ronnie stopped the panic by shouting 'HARD!', meaning 'halt'. The noise could have been the bomb going off, but since it was unaccompanied by shrapnel it seemed safe to pay attention. Everyone turned and looked down. Ronnie picked up the whole mortar, base plate included, shook out the bomb and handed it to Peebles. Silence. Wokka still had his hands over his eyes. Peebles dropped the bomb in the right way up. The mortar coughed. There was a crackle in the sky and a blast on the hill. Then we all marched thoughtfully back to camp.

By now I had made a career out of being a private. Having made the mistake of supplying all the right answers in the intelligence test (since it was exactly the same test that I had been studying in Psychology I, this was no great feat), I was at first put under some pressure to become an officer, or failing that an NCO. But it soon became clear to all concerned that I was a born private. I had revived my joker persona as a means of ingratiating myself with my fellow conscripts. I had no wish to lose their approval by being raised above them. Nor was I morally equipped to accept responsibility for others. But I did manage to get better at being the lowest form of life in the army. I was a digger. I learned the tricks of looking neat without expending too much energy. And although it would have been heresy to say so, I actually enjoyed weapons training. I had the eyes to be good at firing the .303 rifle, but not the hands. Yet I relished being instructed on it. And the Bren was such a perfect machine that there was avid competition to specialize. I never got to the stage of wanting to sleep with one, but must admit that there were times when, as I eyed the Bren's sleek lines, I discovered in myself a strong urge to fiddle with its gas escape regulator.

The weapons sergeants were all regular soldiers with combat experience, usually in Korea. There was virtue, it seemed to me, in listening when they talked. They were wise in their craft. Every few intakes one of them got shot by a National Serviceman. None of them wanted to be the one. After surviving a long encounter with half a million glory-hungry Chinese it makes no sense to be finished off by some adolescent pointing his rifle at you and saying, 'Sergeant, it's stuck.' They were particularly careful when it came to instructing us on the Owen machine carbine. This was the same gun I had once carted around Jannali. The Owen cocked itself if you dropped it and shot you when you picked it up. It disgorged fat, 9mm slugs at a very high rate of fire and the barrel clawed up to the right during the burst. If due precautions were not taken, the man on the left of the line would mow down everyone else, including the instructor. The sergeants were very cautious about whom they put on the left, and always stood well to the left

HENRY LAWSON

The Loaded Dog

Dave Reagan, Jim Bently, and Andy Page were sinking a shaft at Stony Creek in search of a rich gold quartz reef which was supposed to exist in the vicinity. There is always a rich reef supposed to exist in the vicinity; the only questions are whether it is ten feet or hundreds beneath the surface, and in which direction. They had struck some pretty solid rock, also water which kept them bailing. They used the old-fashioned blasting-powder and time-fuse. They'd make a sausage or cartridge of blasting-powder in a skin of strong calico or canvas, the mouth sewn and bound round the end of the fuse; they'd dip the cartridge in melted tallow to make it watertight, get the drill-hole as dry as possible, drop in the cartridge with some dry dust, and wad and ram with stiff clay and broken brick. Then they'd light the fuse and get out of the hole and wait. The result was usually an ugly pot-hole in the bottom of the shaft and half a barrow-load of broken rock.

There was plenty of fish in the creek, fresh-water bream, cod, cat-fish, and tailers. The party were fond of fish, and Andy and Dave of fishing. Andy would fish for three hours at a stretch if encouraged by a nibble or a bite now and then—say once in twenty minutes. The butcher was always willing to give meat in exchange for fish when they caught more than they could eat; but now it was winter, and these fish wouldn't bite. However, the creek was low, just a chain of muddy water-holes, from the hole with a few bucketfuls in it to the sizeable pool with an average depth of six or seven feet, and they could get fish by bailing out the smaller holes or muddying up the water in the larger ones till the fish rose to the surface. There was the cat-fish, with spikes growing out of the sides of its head, and if you got pricked you'd know it, as Dave said. Andy took off his boots, tucked up his trousers, and went into a hole one day to stir up the mud with his feet, and he knew it. Dave themselves. Some of them stood so far to the left they were out of sight. Without exception they refused to let Peebles fire the thing at all. They parked him behind his usual tree on the way to the range and faked his score.

I also enjoyed drill. Einstein once said that any man who liked marching had been given his brain for nothing: just the spinal column would have done. But I wasn't Einstein. Since most of one's time in the army is wasted anyway, I preferred to waste it by moving about in a precise manner. It was better than blueing my pay-packet at a pontoon game in the lavatories. As fit as I would ever be in my life, I could fling a Lee-Enfield .303 rifle around like a baton. When I was ordered to volunteer as Right Front Marker for the exhibition drill squad, I sensibly said yes. Saying no would have immediately entailed being lowered into the big dixie, so it was scarcely a courageous decision.

scooped one out with his hand and got pricked, and he knew it too; his arm swelled, and the pain throbbed up into his shoulder, and down into his stomach, too, he said, like a toothache he had once, and kept him awake for two nights— only the toothache pain had a 'burred edge', Dave said.

Dave got an idea.

'Why not blow the fish up in the big water-hole with a cart-ridge?' he said. 'I'll try it.'

He thought the thing out and Andy Page worked it out. Andy usually put Dave's theories into practice if they were practicable, or bore the blame for the failure and chaffing of his mates if they weren't.

He made a cartridge about three times the size of those they used in the rock. Jim Bently said it was big enough to blow the bottom out of the river. The inner skin was of stout calico; Andy stuck the end of a six-foot piece of fuse well down in the powder and bound the mouth of the bag firmly to it with whipcord. The idea was to sink the cartridge in the water with the open end of the fuse attached to a float on the surface, ready for lighting. Andy dipped the cartridge in melted bees-wax to make it watertight. 'We'll have to leave it some time before we can light it,' said Dave, 'to give the fish time to get over their scare when we put it in, and come nosing round again; so we'll want it well watertight.

Round the cartridge Andy, at Dave's suggestion, bound a strip of sail canvas—that they used for making water-bags—to increase the force of the explosion, and round that he pasted layers of stiff brown paper—on the plan of the sort of fireworks we called 'gun-crackers'. He let the paper dry in the sun, then he sewed a covering of two thicknesses of canvas over it, and bound the thing from end to end with stout fishing line. Dave's schemes were elaborate, and he often worked his inventions out to nothing. The cartridge was rigid and solid enough now—a formidable bomb; but Andy and Dave wanted to be sure. Andy sewed on another layer of canvas, dipped the cartridge in melted tallow, twisted a length of fen-cing wire round it as an afterthought, dipped it in tallow again, and stood it carefully against a tent-peg, where he'd know where to find it, and wound the fuse loosely round it.

Then he went to the camp-fire to try some potatoes which were boiling in their jackets in a billy, and to see about frying some chops for dinner. Dave and Jim were at work in the claim that morning.

They had a big black young retriever dog—or rather an overgrown pup, a big, foolish, four-footed mate, who was always slobbering round them and lashing their legs with his heavy tail that swung round like a stockwhip. Most of his head was usually a red, idiotic slobbering grin of appreciation of his own silliness. He seemed to take life, the world, his two-legged mates, and his own instinct as a huge joke. He'd retrieve anything; he carted back most of the camp rubbish that Andy threw away. They had a cat that died in hot weather, and Andy threw it a good distance away in the scrub; and early one morning the dog found the cat, after it had been dead a week or so, and carried it back to camp, and laid it just inside the tent-flaps, where it could best make its presence known when the mates should rise and begin to sniff suspiciously in the sickly smothering atmosphere of the summer sunrise. He used to retrieve them when they went in swimming; he'd jump in after them, and scratch their naked bodies with his paws. They loved him for his good-heartedness and his foolishness, but when they wished to enjoy a swim they had to tie him up in camp.

He watched Andy with great interest all the morning making the cartridge, and hindered him considerably, trying to help; but about noon he went off to the claim to see how Dave and Jim were getting on, and to come home to dinner with them. Andy saw them coming, and put a panful of mutton-chops on the fire. Andy was cook today; Dave and Jim stood with their backs to the fire, as bushmen do in all weathers, waiting till dinner should be ready. The retriever went nosing round after something he seemed to have missed.

Andy's brain still worked on the cartridge; his eye was caught by the glare of an empty kerosene-tin lying in the bushes, and it struck him that it wouldn't be a bad idea to sink the cartridge packed with clay, sand, or stones in the tin, to increase the force of the explosion. He may have been all out, from a scientific point of view, but the notion looked all right to him. Jim Bently, by the way, wasn't interested in their 'damned silliness'. Andy noticed an empty treacle-tin—the sort with the little tin neck or spout soldered on to the top for the convenience of pouring out the treacle—and it struck him that this would have made the best kind of cartridge-case: he would only have had to pour in the powder, stick the fuse in through the neck, and cork and seal it with beeswax. He was turning to suggest this to Dave, when Dave glanced over his shoulder to see how the chops were doing—and bolted. He explained afterwards that he thought he heard the pan sputtering extra, and looked to see if the chops were burning. Jim Bently looked behind him and bolted after Dave. Andy stood stock-still, staring after them.

'Run, Andy! Run!' they shouted back at him. 'Run! Look behind you, you fool!' Andy turned slowly and looked, and there, close behind him, was the retriever with the cartridge in his mouth—wedged into his broadest and silliest grin. And that wasn't all. The dog had come round the fire to Andy, and the loose end of the fuse had trailed and waggled over the burning sticks into the blaze; Andy had slit and nicked the firing end of the fuse well, and now it was hissing and spitting properly.

Andy's legs started with a jolt; his legs started before his brain did, and he made after Dave and Jim. And the dog followed Andy.

Dave and Jim were good runners—Jim the best—for a short distance; Andy was slow and heavy, but he had the strength and the wind and could last. The dog capered round him, delighted as a dog could be to find his mates, as he thought, on for a frolic. Dave and Jim shouted back, 'Don't foller us! Don't foller us, you coloured fool!' But Andy kept on, no matter how they dodged. They could never explain, any more than the dog, why they followed each other, but so they ran, Dave keeping in Jim's track in all its turnings, Andy after Dave, and the dog circling round Andy—the live fuse swishing in all directions and hissing and spluttering and stinking. Jim yelling to Dave not to follow him, Dave shouting to Andy to go in another direction—to 'spread out', and Andy roaring at the dog to go home. Then Andy's brain began to work, stimulated by the crisis: he tried to get a running kick at the dog, but the dog dodged; he snatched up sticks and stones and threw them at the dog and ran on again. The retriever saw that he'd made a mistake about Andy, and left him and bounded after Dave. Dave, who had the presence of mind to think that the fuse's time wasn't up yet, made a dive and a grab for the dog, caught him by the tail, and as he swung round snatched the cartridge out of his mouth and flung it as far as he could; the dog immediately bounded after it and retrieved it. Dave roared and cursed at the dog, who, seeing that Dave was offended, left him and went after Jim who was well ahead. Jim swung to a sapling and went up it like a native bear; it was a young sapling, and Jim couldn't safely get more than ten or twelve feet from the ground. The dog laid the cartridge, as carefully as if it were a kitten, at the foot of the sapling, and capered and leaped and whooped joyously round under Jim. The big pup reckoned that this was part of the lark—he was all right now—it was Jim who was out for a spree. The fuse sounded as if it were going a mile a minute. Jim tried to climb higher and the sapling bent and cracked. Jim fell on his feet and ran. The dog swooped on the cartridge and followed. It all took but a very few moments. Jim ran to a digger's hole, about ten feet deep, and dropped down into it—landing on soft mud—and was safe. The dog grinned sardonically down on him, over the edge, for a moment, as if he thought it would be a good lark to drop the cartridge down on Jim.

'Go away, Tommy,' said Jim feebly, 'go away.'

The dog bounded off after Dave, who was the only one in sight now; Andy had dropped behind a log, where he lay flat on his face, having suddenly remembered a picture of the Russo-Turkish war with a circle of Turks lying flat on their faces (as if they were ashamed) round a newly-arrived shell.

There was a small hotel or shanty on the creek, on the main road, not far from the claim. Dave was desperate, and time flew much faster in his stimulated imagination than it did in reality, so he made for the shanty. There were several casual bushmen on the veranda and in the bar; Dave rushed into the bar, banging the door to behind him. 'My dog!' he gasped, in reply to the astonished stare of the publican, 'the blanky retriever—he's got a live cartridge in his mouth—'

The retriever, finding the front door shut against him, had bounded round and in by the back way, and now stood smiling in the doorway leading from the passage, the cartridge still in his mouth and the fuse spluttering. They burst out of that bar; Tommy bounded first after one and then after another, for, being a young dog, he tried to make friends with everybody.

The bushmen ran round corners, and some shut themselves in the stable. There was a new weatherboard and corrugated-iron kitchen and wash-house on piles in the backyard, with some women washing clothes inside. Dave and the publican bundled in there and shut the door—the publican cursing Dave and calling him a crimson fool, in hurried tones, and wanting to know what the hell he came here for.

The retriever went in under the kitchen, amongst the piles, but, luckily for those inside, there was a vicious yellow mongrel cattle-dog sulking and nursing his nastiness under there—a sneaking, fighting, thieving canine, whom neighbours had tried for years to shoot or poison. Tommy saw his danger—he'd had experience from this dog—and started out and across the yard, still sticking to the cartridge. Half-way across the yard the yellow dog caught him and nipped him. Tommy dropped the cartridge, gave one terrified yell and took to the bush. The yellow dog followed him to the fence and then ran back to see what he had dropped. Nearly a dozen other dogs came from round all the corners and under the buildings—spidery, thievish, cold-blooded kangaroo-dogs, mongrel sheep- and cattle-dogs, vicious black and yellow dogs—that slip after you in the dark, nip your heels, and vanish without explaining—yapping, yelping small fry. They kept a respectable distance round the nasty yellow dog, for it was dangerous to go near him when he thought he had found something which might be good for a dog or cat. He sniffed at the cartridge twice, and was just taking a third cautious sniff when—

It was very good blasting-powder—a new brand that Dave had recently got up from Sydney; and the cartridge had been excellently well made. Andy was very patient and painstaking in all he did, and nearly as handy as the average sailor with needles, twine, canvas and rope.

Bushmen say that that kitchen jumped off its piles and on again. When the smoke and dust cleared away, the remains of the nasty yellow dog were lying against the paling fence of the yard looking as if it had been kicked into a fire by a horse and afterwards rolled in the dust under a barrow, and finally thrown against the fence from a distance. Several saddle-horses, which had been 'hanging-up' round the veranda, were galloping wildly down the road in clouds of dust, with broken bridle-reins flying; and from a circle round the out-skirts, from every point of the compass in the scrub, came the yelping of dogs. Two of them went home, to the place where they were born, thirty miles away, and reached it the same night and stayed there; it was not till towards evening that the rest came back cautiously to make inquiries. One was trying to walk on two legs, and most of 'em looked more or less singed; and a little, singed, stumpy-tailed dog, who had been in the habit of hopping the back half of him along on one leg, had reason to be glad that he'd saved up the other leg all those years, for he needed it now. There was one old one-eyed cattle-dog round the shanty for years afterwards, who couldn't stand the smell of a gun being cleaned. He it was who had taken an interest only second to that of the yellow dog, in the cartridge. Bushmen said that it was amusing to slip up on his blind side and stick a dirty ramrod under his nose: he wouldn't wait to bring his solitary eye to bear—he'd take to the bush and stay out all night.

For half an hour or so after the explosion there were several bushmen round behind the stable who crouched, doubled up, against the wall, or rolled gently on the dust, trying to laugh without shrieking. There were two white women in hysterics at the house, and a half-caste rushing aimlessly round with a dipper of cold water. The publican was holding his wife tight and begging her between her squawks, to 'Hold up for my sake, Mary, or I'll lam the life out of ye!'

Dave decided to apologize later on, 'when things had set-tled a bit', and went back to camp. And the dog that had done it all, Tommy, the great, idiotic mongrel retriever, came slob-

bering round Dave and lashing his legs with his tail, and trot-
ted home after him, smiling his broadest, longest, and reddest
smile of amiability, and apparently satisfied for one afternoon
with the fun he'd had.

Andy chained the dog up securely, and cooked some more
chops, while Dave went to help Jim out of the hole.

And most of this is why, for years afterwards, lanky, easy-
going bushmen, riding lazily past Dave's camp, would cry, in
a lazy drawl and with just a hint of the nasal twang:

"Ello, Da-a-ve! How's the fishin' getting on, Da-a-ve?'

Daily Dilemmas

If I take a soft drink,
I get the sugar,
calories, and cavities.

If I drink Lo-Cal,
I get saccharin or cyclamates
and a chance at cancer.

I'm not always sure
whether I'd rather
die young but thin
or old and fat.

Natasha Josefowitz

The Diet

Sat in the pub
Drink flowing free
Everyone's merry
Cept poor old me
I'm starving

I have to sit
in the corner
All quiet
The trouble you see
I'm on a diet
I'm starving

No whisky, no gin
Why did I come in
no ploughman's lunch
like that greedy bunch
I'm starving

Shall I walk to the bar
I won't go too far
Just a pkt of crisps
and one drink
I'm starving

Then I think I'll have
when I've finished this fag
some chicken and chips
in a basket
I'm starving

No I can't keep quiet
I'll shout, Bugger the diet
I'm absolutely starving

Maureen Burge

E322—
or Is My Mother Trying to Kill Me?

I don't have school dinners:
My mum packs up a box,
So I scoff my sarnies in the Hall—
Watch the others getting spots.
I have brown bread with bits in
Spread with soya marg and cheese,
I just stare at chips and custard,
The batter and the peas . . .
I get a balanced diet
Don't stuff myself with starch,
Protect my teeth from sugar,
Keep them strong and sharp.

But today she put a biscuit
In with all my grub
A chocolate covered biscuit:
A symbol of her love.
I idly read the packet
Saw what they'd put inside.
I read the wrapper once again
And then I nearly died!

There's emulsifier E322,
the sugar and the flour,
whey powder, glucose syrup,
colouring (110, 102, 150) & some malt,
cocoa (fat reduced),
milk chocolate flavouring
—would you believe?—
antioxidant 320
and a bit of bleeding salt!

I read it through just one more time,
I gulped, and then I thought:

SHE'S TRYING TO KILL ME!

But I ate it anyway and I'm not de$_a$$_d$

$$y \quad _e$$

$$t$$

.

Trevor Millum

Giving Up Smoking

There's not a Shakespeare sonnet
Or a Beethoven quartet
That's easier to like than you
Or harder to forget.

You think that sounds extravagant?
I haven't finished yet—
I like you more than I would like
To have a cigarette.

Wendy Cope

Goat's Tobacco

When I was about nine, the ancient half-sister got engaged to be married. The man of her choice was a young English doctor and that summer he came with us to Norway. Romance was floating in the air like moondust and the two lovers, for some reason we younger ones could never understand, did not seem to be very keen on us tagging along with them. They went out in the boat alone. They climbed the rocks alone. They even had breakfast alone. We resented this. As a family we had always done everything together and we didn't see why the ancient half-sister should suddenly decide to do things differently even if she had become engaged. We were inclined to blame the male lover for disrupting the calm of our family life, and it was inevitable that he would have to suffer for it sooner or later.

The male lover was a great pipe-smoker. The disgusting smelly pipe was never out of his mouth except when he was eating or swimming. We even began to wonder whether he removed it when he was kissing his betrothed. He gripped the stem of the pipe in the most manly fashion between his strong white teeth and kept it there while taking to you. This annoyed us. Surely it was more polite to take it out and speak properly.

One day, we all went in our little motor-boat to an island we had never been to before, and for once the ancient half-sister and the manly lover decided to come with us. We chose this particular island because we saw some goats on it. They were climbing about on the rocks and we thought it would be fun to go and visit them. But when we landed, we found that the goats were totally wild and we couldn't get near them. So we gave up trying to make friends with them and simply sat around on the smooth rocks in our bathing costumes, enjoying the lovely sun.

34

The manly lover was filling his pipe. I happened to be watching him as he very carefully packed the tobacco into the bowl from a yellow oilskin pouch. He had just finished doing this and was about to light up when the ancient half-sister called on him to come swimming. So he put down the pipe and off he went.

I stared at the pipe that was lying there on the rocks. About twelve inches away from it, I saw a little heap of dried goat's droppings, each one small and round like a pale brown berry, and at that point, an interesting idea began to sprout in my mind. I picked up the pipe and knocked all the tobacco out of it. I then took the goat's droppings and teased them with my fingers until they were nicely shredded. Very gently I poured these shredded droppings into the bowl of the pipe, packing them down with my thumb just as the manly lover always did it. When that was done, I placed a thin layer of real tobacco over the top. The entire family was watching me as I did this. Nobody said a word, but I could sense a glow of approval all round. I replaced the pipe on the rock, and all of us sat back to await the return of the victim. The whole lot of us were in this together now, even my mother. I had drawn them into the plot simply by letting them see what I was doing. It was a silent, rather dangerous family conspiracy.

Back came the manly lover, dripping wet from the sea, chest out, strong and virile, healthy and sunburnt. 'Great swim!' he announced to the world. 'Splendid water! Terrific stuff!' He towelled himself vigorously, making the muscles of his biceps ripple, then he sat down on the rocks and reached for his pipe.

Nine pairs of eyes watched him intently. Nobody giggled to give the game away. We were trembling with anticipation, and a good deal of the suspense was caused by the fact that none of us knew just what was going to happen.

The manly lover put the pipe between his strong white teeth and struck a match. He held the flame over the bowl and sucked. The tobacco ignited and glowed, and the lover's head was enveloped in clouds of blue smoke. 'Ah-h-h,' he said, blowing smoke through his nostrils. 'There's nothing like a good pipe after a bracing swim.'

Still we waited. We could hardly bear the suspense. The sister who was seven couldn't bear it at all. 'What *sort* of tobacco do you put in that thing?' she asked with superb innocence.

'Navy Cut,' the male lover answered. 'Player's Navy Cut. It's the best there is. These Norwegians use all sorts of disgusting scented tobaccos, but I wouldn't touch them.'

'I didn't know they had different tastes,' the small sister went on.

'Of course they do,' the manly lover said. 'All tobaccos are different to the discriminating pipe-smoker. Navy Cut is clean and unadulterated. It's a man's smoke.' The man seemed to go out of his way to use long words like discriminating and unadulterated. We hadn't the foggiest what they meant.

The ancient half-sister, fresh from her swim and now clothed in a towel bathrobe, came and sat herself close to her manly lover. Then the two of them started giving each other those silly little glances and soppy smiles that made us all feel sick. They were far too occupied with one another to notice the awful tension that had settled over our group. They didn't even notice that every face in the crowd was turned towards them. They had sunk once again into their lovers' world where little children did not exist.

The sea was calm, the sun was shining and it was a beautiful day.

Then all of a sudden, the manly lover let out a piercing scream and his whole body shot four feet into the air. His pipe flew out of his mouth and went clattering over the rocks, and the second scream he gave was so shrill and loud that all the seagulls on the island rose up in alarm. His features were twisted like those of a person undergoing severe torture, and his skin had turned the colour of snow. He began spluttering and choking and spewing and hawking and acting generally like a man with some serious internal injury. He was completely speechless.

We stared at him, enthralled.

The ancient half-sister, who must have thought she was about to lose her future husband for ever, was pawing at him and thumping him on the back and crying, 'Darling! Darling! What's happening to you? Where does it hurt? Get the boat! Start the engine! We must rush him to a hospital quickly!' She

36

seemed to have forgotten that there wasn't a hospital within fifty miles.

'I've been poisoned!' spluttered the manly lover. 'It's got into my lungs! It's in my chest! My chest is on fire! My stomach's going up in flames!'

'Help me get him into the boat! Quick!' cried the ancient half-sister, gripping him under the armpits. 'Don't just sit there staring! Come and help!'

'No, no, no!' cried the now not-so-manly lover. 'Leave me alone! I need air! Give me air!' He lay back and breathed in deep draughts of splendid Norwegian ocean air, and in another minute or so, he was sitting up again and was on the way to recovery.

'What in the world came over you?' asked the ancient half-sister, clasping his hands tenderly in hers.

'I can't imagine,' he murmured. 'I simply can't imagine.' His face was as still and white as virgin snow and his hands were trembling. 'There must be a reason for it,' he added. 'There's got to be a reason.'

'I know the reason!' shouted the seven-year-old sister, screaming with laughter. 'I know what it was!'

'What was it?' snapped the ancient one. 'What have you been up to? Tell me at once!'

'It's his pipe!' shouted the small sister, still convulsed with laughter.

'What's wrong with my pipe?' said the manly lover.

'You've been smoking goat's tobacco!' cried the small sister.

It took a few moments for the full meaning of these words to dawn upon the two lovers, but when it did, and when the terrible anger began to show itself on the manly lover's face, and when he started to rise slowly and menacingly to his feet, we all sprang up and ran for our lives and jumped off the rocks into the deep water.

W*here Did our Pete Find this Tiger?*

The writer is one of six children, writing about her childhood in a Midlands town in 1948. The other children are Pete, Tone, Lucy, Rose and Joe and there's a dog called Prince.

I think it's just as well I went to Sunday School yesterday because I got run over today. See what I mean about Guardian Angels though, don't you? I mean, where was mine at the time, that's what I'd like to know?

I'm lying on the sofa writing this. Our Mam says I've aged her ten years in a day. I don't know why they always get on at me. It's not my fault. I was just crossing the road and this motor-bike ran over me. So I laid there and this lad jumped off and he's shouting, 'Oh! Oh! What have I done? What have I done?' and I looked up at him and I said, 'You've blooming well run over me, that's what you've done!' and I sat up and then I opened my mouth and started yelling because there was all blood down my legs and it was dripping off my hands and when I touched my face that was bleeding as well.

Our Mam came rushing out of the house like a reindeer, and she picks me up and rushes back with me and lays me on the sofa and before you can move, the kitchen's full of everybody in the street. I bet you can't guess who were at the front of the queue though? Yes, that's right. Old Flo and Granny Bates and Mrs Elston. Mrs Elston says, 'I think I'm going to be sick,' and Old Flo says to her, 'If you're going to be sick, you go off home and be sick in your own house, my girl,' and Mrs Elston screwed up her mouth and said, 'Well, it's passed off now,' and she stayed.

Old Flo and Granny Bates were ever so nice. Old Flo got a big basin of water and she bathed all my legs and arms and all my face. It hurt like mad, but what I was really crying for was because my new Whit Sunday frock had a tear in it. Our Mam says, 'Shush, shush, my little lass,' and she starts blinking her eyes very fast and I thought, 'Oh, she's going to cry,' so I started crying, which I always do when our Mam cries because I can't help it. And then, Old Flo says to our Mam, 'There, there, now. Look Gran's got you a nice cup of tea,' and our Mam kept saying, 'I don't want no tea. Fetch a doctor,' and Old Flo says, 'We've sent for him but there's nothing broken. She'll be all right,' and I thought, there she goes again. She'll ask me to get up and mend the fire next, but she didn't.

Anyway, when the doctor came, it was all over, bar the shouting, and our Dad was doing plenty of that because that young lad on the bike couldn't drive and he'd borrowed the bike from his mate and there were bobbies outside and everything. What a carry on.

The nice doctor came, the one with the cool hands, and he looked at me and then at our Mam and he said, 'How many children have you got?' Our Mam said, 'Six,' and he said, 'I thought it was six. Why is it always this one that gets into bother?' and our Mam smiled at him, just a little smile, and then she says, 'She's been more trouble than the other five put together and that's a fact.' I thought, 'What a thing to say,' and I felt really fed up, so I started crying again, and then our Mam hugged me and said, 'But I wouldn't part with her for a five-pound note.' So then I stopped crying and felt a lot better.

The doctor gave me some medicine and I fell asleep. I've only just woken up again. All our lads and our Lucy and Rose bought me sweets and some comics and our Dad even gave me some grapes, which I gave to Mam, but she made me eat them, which I'm glad about because they were ever so good.

Our Mam says my new frock will mend just like new again. Old Flo and Granny Bates have been sat in the kitchen all day and every time they think I can hear what they're talking about, one of them looks over at me and says, 'Now shush, my little lass,' and I have to close my eyes again and pretend to be asleep. I shall be glad when I can get up. I don't like being in bed and I've been on this sofa all day.

I was glad when our Pete got home tonight. He'd brought a rabbit home from the farm with him. It's a real big one. I thought it was still alive and I said to him, 'Can I hold it?' and he said, 'All right' and when he gave it me, it was dead. I screamed my head off and our Mam said, 'You'd think you'd have more sense at your age,' and our Pete said, 'Well, I'll bring her a kitten tomorrow. The farm cat's just had a litter.' So our Mam said, 'That's all right then.' But I thought, I don't want a kitten. It might scratch our Prince. Prince is our dog and I love him. But then nobody ever asks me what I want because I'm only a *child*.

Our Mam looked at the rabbit and she said, 'That'll make a nice stew,' and I said to her, 'I don't want none, Mam,' and she said, 'Don't you be so foolish, my lass. You're having some whether you want it or not,' and I thought, when I grow up, I shall never eat anything I don't want in all my life.

So, that poor little rabbit had to be made into a stew and our Pete said, 'Well, it might as well go into a stew, mightn't it, 'cos it couldn't run about and play any more, could it?' And I said to him, 'Did you kill it?' and he said, 'No,' and I said, 'Well, how did it get to be dead then?' and he said, 'It died of old age, my old love,' and I said, 'Oh, well, that's different then. I'll eat some if it died of old age.'

'Yes,' he said. 'I was standing there, in the middle of this field, and I sees this rabbit coming towards me.' He looked at me to see if I was listening properly because he likes you to listen properly, our Pete, and not just keep saying, 'Yes, yes,' and not listen at all. 'Go on,' I said, 'I'm listening,' and he went on, 'And I watched it and I thought, by, there's something queer about that rabbit and then I saw what it was.'

'What was it?' I asked, and he said, 'I don't rightly know if I should tell you,' and I shouted, 'Maaaaammmmm,' and he said, 'Oh, all right then. So, I sees what's wrong with it. It's walking on a pair of crutches.' I looked at him and he looked at me and he said, 'Well, do you want me to go on?' and I said, 'I think so,' and he went on, 'Well, there it is, on these crutches, and it got right up to my feet and I heard it say, "Oh, by gum, I can't step over them hills," and it fell over backwards, with its paws in the air. So I picked it up and I says to it, "Are you all right?" and it says, "Nay lad, I'm not, and I were just on way to Post Office for me pension as well." '

40

So, I looked at our Pete and he looked at me and he said, 'What do you reckon to that?' and I said, 'I reckon I'm not as daft as I look,' and he laughed and said, 'Well, anyway, I'll bring you that kitten tomorrow.'

So now I'm going to get a kitten I don't want and every time it widdles on the floor, everybody will shout at *me* and say, 'It's your kitten. You should clean up after it,' and I'll spend all my entire life, knee-deep in disinfectant and floor cloths and newspaper just like I did with our Prince. But I love our Prince and I never minded doing it for him. I don't feel like doing it for a kitten though.

We had rabbit stew and dumplings for dinner and I kept seeing that poor old rabbit with its paws in the air talking to our Pete. Our Mam nearly went mad with our Pete. 'Why won't you eat it?' she said, and I told her about it going to collect its pension on crutches and she started laughing and then she said to our Pete, 'You'll have to buy her something from the shop,' and he said, 'I've only got enough money for the pictures, Mam,' and she said, 'You should have thought of that before you tormented her,' and he moaned and groaned until in the end I said, 'Oh, I feel like my stew now, Mam,' and she brought it out of the oven and said to our Pete, 'And you may think yourself very lucky, my lad,' and our Pete actually patted my head—yuk, yuk, yuk. Next time, I won't eat it and then he'll have to spend his picture money.

They're all scraping up money to go out with tonight, and because I'm downstairs I have to lie here and watch them get ready. First our Pete and then our Tone. Our Pete put so much brilliantine on his hair I said to him, 'If ever you fell on your head, you'd slide down the street,' and he said I'd rattle more than an empty tin can. 'Empty tin cans don't rattle,' I said. 'They do when you kick them,' he said and glared at me. So I thought I'd better keep quiet for a bit.

Our Tone took about seventeen hours to get ready. Even our Mam said, 'I've never known anybody take so long getting ready to go anywhere before. If you were getting wed you couldn't take much longer.' Our Lucy said, 'Oh, haven't you heard? He's got a girl-friend as well now,' and our Tone jumped across the kitchen with the flannel in his hand and he

41

stuffed it down our Lucy's back. She wasn't half mad. She was crying she was so mad.

Our Mam says to her, 'Now, it serves you right for tale telling,' and our Lucy said, 'I wasn't tale telling. I was only . . . '

'Tale telling!' our Tone yelled at her.

Our Lucy sniffed and said to our Mam, 'If you wouldn't mind taking that wet flannel from out of my jumper, Mother,' and she just stood there scowling at our Tone. I thought, poor old Tone. I bet something pretty horrible's going to happen to you, because she's a rum one to cross, our Lucy.

Anyway, they all went out at last and we were sat there, me and our Mam and Dad and Rose and Joe, listening to a ghost story on the wireless. Our Mam blew out the gas lamp and we were sat in the firelight and it was real still and spooky, when all of a sudden there was this terrible screaming and yelling in the passage. You could tell it was in the passage because when you make a noise in there, it echoes.

'Whatever's that?' our Mam shouted, and she was scrambling around for matches to light the gas mantle and she kept shouting to our Dad, 'Go and see who it is, John! Go on! Quickly!' and our Dad shot up out of his chair saying, 'All right, Lissy, all right. Don't panic! Don't panic!' to our Mam, because he was half asleep. He'd dropped off sitting there all quiet and waking up so sudden, he hardly knew where he was.

So, our Dad shakes his head, marches through the kitchen, picks up his big torch and flings open the back door. He shines the torch down the passage and we're all trying to see round him and there's our Tone and Lucy rolling over and over down the passage, and standing against the wall like a weed is a tall, thin girl. She's going, 'Ooooh! Ooooh!' and our Dad strides down the passage and gives me the torch to hold.

First, he hauls our Lucy to her feet and then our Tone and he has to hold them apart because they're both still trying to get at each other. 'I'll kill you,' our Tone roars and our Lucy laughs in just the way our Tone hates. 'Ha, ha!' she goes. 'You and whose army?' Our Dad drags them both up the passage and into the back yard.

By now all the back doors are open and everybody in the

street seems to be in the yard. Mrs Elston shouts to our Lucy, 'That's right, my girl, stand up for your rights,' and our Mam says to her, 'Oh yes, you encourage her to behave like a hooligan, I should,' and she marches over to our Lucy and says to her, 'In!' Our Lucy takes one look at our Mam's face and she goes all quiet and walks into the house.

Our Dad says to Tone, 'I think you'd better go in as well, lad,' and our Tone nods. Then our Dad says, 'Is that little lass with you?' and he looks at this tall, thin girl who's still standing against the wall in the passage. Tone says, 'Yes,' and our Dad says, 'Go and get her then. You'll have some explaining to do there, I shouldn't wonder.' Our Mam says, 'Not as much as he's going to have to do in that house,' and she waits till our Tone fetches this girl up the passage and then we all go into the house and our Mam shuts the back door. Bang!

We're all crowded into the room and I get back on the sofa before our Mam sees I'm walking around. I see this tall, thin girl is crying. There's all tears falling down her face. It's the first time I've seen anybody cry without making a noise.

'Now,' says our Mam. 'What happened?' Our Tone is scowling and our Lucy's face is as white as a sheet and her lips are all tight when she's not talking, but when she tries to say anything they go quiver, quiver. This other girl is standing there and she suddenly points at our Lucy and says, 'It was her!' Our Mam turns round and looks at Lucy and Lucy sort of shrugs her shoulders and screws up her face and says, 'Well,' and then it all came out.

Our Lucy had followed Tone to the pictures and sat behind him and his girl-friend and just when they were kissing and cuddling each other, she stuffed an ice cream down the back of his shirt, but half of it went into his girl-friend's ear and they'd all been thrown out of the pictures because of the noise. They'd even stopped the film in the middle and turned on the lights because our Tone was chasing Lucy up and down the aisles.

I should have liked to have seen that and our Mam says to me, 'You stop laughing else you'll go straight up to bed, poorly or no poorly.' So I shut up and got right down under the covers where they couldn't see if I was laughing or not.

Anyway, it all ended up with our Lucy being made to pay for a new shirt for our Tone out of her paper money that she gets for taking out the papers in the night and morning, which will keep her at home for the next month, our Mam said, and our Tone having to say he was sorry to that girl and our Lucy having to say she was sorry to that girl as well.

Then, our Mam said it was time for some supper and she said to the girl, 'Do you want some supper, love?' and the girl said, 'I'd rather go home, I think,' and our Tone put his fist up at Lucy and luckily for him, our Mam didn't see it.

That girl went out saying to our Mam, 'I've never been so ashamed in all my life,' and I looked at our Lucy and she looked at me and I said to her, 'I don't like her either,' and Lucy grinned and said, 'I shouldn't have done that, though,' and went to bed before our Mam came back.

But that was no good and I could have told her so because all that happened then was our Mam said, 'And where is that little madam?' and I said, 'I'm here, Mam,' because usually it's me she calls that. She smiles at me and says, 'Just for once, it's not you,' and I said, 'I don't know where she is,' and she says, 'I'll find her,' and she went straight upstairs and didn't come down again for ages.

My legs hurt that much from where that motorbike ran over them that I couldn't get to sleep that night and every time our Lucy and Rose moved, they kicked me. So in the end I woke our Mam up and she said, 'Come on. I'll make you a bed up on the sofa,' so me and our Mam slept downstairs in the front room all night. Our Mam slept in the big old armchair and when it was half-past five, she went and shouted our Pete up. He came tumbling down the stairs as if he'd got his eyes shut.

'What's up, my old love?' he says to me when he saw me lying on the sofa and I told him my legs hurt. 'That kitten'll be very nice then, won't it?' he says and I says, 'What about our Prince?' and our Pete says, 'Well, what about him?' and I says, 'He doesn't like cats,' and our Pete starts getting mad then and saying, 'If you don't want a kitten, just say so.' So I said, 'I don't want one,' and he went, 'Oh! Oh! Never grateful, people in this house aren't,' and then he says, 'Well, you're getting one anyway, whether you want one or not,' and I thought,

'Boy, I'll be glad when I'm better and nobody wants to bring me things any more.'

Anyway, our Pete slammed out of the back door and our Mam says, 'Why don't you want a kitten?' and I says, 'I don't really like them, Mam,' and our Mam says, 'Well, you're a funny one, aren't you?' and everybody in the whole wide world seems to agree with that.

Anyway, I was lying there wondering why people can't fly, because it would be very handy when you'd hurt your legs if you could fly, when our Pete comes back for his breakfast and hanging from his hand was this old brown sack with a lump in it and the lump was going 'Spit! Spit! Psssst! Yowl! Grrrr!' and our Mam looks at the sack and she says, 'What's that?' and our Pete says, 'It's that kitten for madam there, for a pet for her,' and our Mam said, 'Are you sure?' and our Pete says, 'Why? Why?' and our Mam says, 'Oh, nothing, nothing. Only it doesn't sound very happy, does it?' Personally, I thought it sounded as if it had gone mad, but nobody asked me, of course.

Our Pete walks over to me and he upturns this sack and this kitten drops out on to my knee. I thought it was a baby tiger the way it carried on. It spat and scratched and clawed me until I had to let it go. It's all striped, as well, and it looks like a tiger.

Our Mam looked at it and then she looked at my arms which were covered in scratches and she said, 'Are you sure it's all right?' and our Pete said, 'Of course it's all right. It's *her.*' (pointing at me), 'She doesn't know how to handle them.' 'Oooooh!! Make way for Jungle Boy,' I said.

By now the kitten was swinging along the top of the curtains and our Mam says to Pete, 'Get it down from there, it's tearing all my curtains,' and our Pete reached up for it and it went, 'Pssst!' and he jumped back as if he'd been shot. I laughed like a drain but I soon stopped when our Mam said, 'As you think it's so funny, you get it down,' and I tried and the rotten thing bit me.

I screamed blue murder and our Dad came in from work and said, 'Why is she always screaming when I come home?' and our Mam had just started saying, 'Whatever do you mean, always screaming?' when the kitten swung across the curtains and made a jump for the mantelpiece and our Dad looked at it and said, 'I don't believe it,' and our Mam said, 'It's true. It won't come down and it's bitten madam there and scratched our Pete.' So our Dad said, 'Leave it to me,' and he went to get it and trod accidentally on our Prince who'd just poked his nose out from under the table to see if he'd imagined hearing a cat in the house. Our Dad went flying and our Prince went scuttering round the table howling his poor little head off.

'You big bully,' I shouted at our Dad and our Mam reached over and slapped my arm. 'Well, he is,' I yelled and I had to pick our poor old Prince up and love him better. Our Dad sat on the sofa and he kept saying, 'If ever a man suffered,' and our Mam snapped at our Pete to get that cat out of the house, but we couldn't catch it.

We got it down in the end because our brilliant Pete threw an old towel over it and it was hissing and scratching inside it and our Mam looked at Pete and said, 'And you brought that home as a pet?' Our Pete said, 'It was *her* that done it,' and I said, 'Oh yes, blame me, it's always me,' (which they always say it is).

Anyway, our Dad said, 'You'd better take it back to the farm,' so our Pete took it back after he'd had his breakfast and the farmer said to our Dad when he saw him later that he'd told our Pete his farm cats were really spiteful and he didn't think it would do as a pet, but our Pete wouldn't be told.

'And that's the trouble,' our Dad said when he'd finished telling our Mam the story. 'They never will be told, any of them. We were never like that when we were kids,' and I thought, Oh heck, here we go again, and our Dad goes on and on about how they were all so wonderful when they were little kids.

They sound really horrible to me and I don't know how they ever got to make any friends, they were so good. Although I don't have many friends at all—any friends I suppose—and our Rose always says, 'That's because you're so bad, it's more trouble than it's worth to be friends with you.' So I don't know.

HELEN CRESSWELL

Snake in the Grass

Robin could tell, right from the beginning, that he was going to enjoy the picnic. To begin with, Uncle Joe and Auntie Joy had brought him a present, a bugle.

He took a long, testing blow. The note went on and on and on—and on. He saw Auntie Joy shudder and his cousin Nigel put his hands to his ears. Nigel was twelve, and Robin hardly even came up to his shoulder.

'We'll be off now,' Uncle Joe said, climbing into his car. 'See you there.'

Robin got into the back seat of his father's car.

'It's lovely at Miller's Beck,' his mother said. 'You'll love it, Robin.'

Robin did not reply. The picnic hamper was on the back seat, too, and he was trying to squint between the wickerwork to see what was in there. In the end he gave up squinting, and sniffed. Ham, was it? Tomatoes? Oranges, definitely, and was it—could it be—strawberries?

He sat back and began to practise the bugle. He kept playing the same three notes over and over again, and watched the back of his father's neck turning a dark red.

'D'ye *have* to play that thing now?' he growled at last. 'We shall all end up in a ditch!'

'I'm only trying to learn it, Dad,' said Robin. 'I've always wanted a bugle.'

An hour later, when they reached Miller's Beck, he had invented a tune that he really liked and had already played it about a hundred times. It was a kind of cross between 'Onward Christian Soldiers' and 'My Old Man's a Dustman.'

The minute the car stopped Robin got out and ran down to the stream. He pulled off his shoes and socks and paddled in. The water was icy cold and clear as tap water, running over stones and gravel and small boulders.

Robin began to paddle downstream after a piece of floating bark he wanted for a boat, when,

'Ooooooooch!' he yelled. 'Owwwwch!'

A sharp pain ran through his foot. He balanced on one leg and lifted the hurt foot out of the water. He could see blood dripping from it.

'Ooooowh!' he yelled again. 'Help!'

He began to sway round and round on his good leg, like a spinning top winding down. He threw out his arms, yelled again and was down, flat on his bottom in the icy beck.

'Robin!' he heard his father scream. 'Robin!'

He sat where he was with the water above his waist and the hurt foot lifted above the water, still dripping blood. He couldn't even feel the foot any more. He just sat and stared at it as if it belonged to somebody else.

His father was pulling off his shoes and socks and next minute was splashing in beside him and had lifted him clean up out of the water. Robin clutched him hard and water squelched between them. Robin's elbow moved sharply and he heard his father's yell.

'Hey, my glasses.'

Robin twisted his head and saw first that he was dripping blood all over his father's trousers, second that the bottoms of his father's trousers were in the water because he hadn't had time to roll them up, and third that lying at the bottom of the beck were his father's spectacles. Robin could see at a glance that they were broken—at least, one of the lenses was.

His father staggered blindly out of the water, smack into Uncle Joe who was hopping on the bank.

'Here! Take him!' he gasped.

Then Robin was in Uncle Joe's arms, dripping blood and water all over *him*, and was carried back up the slope with his mother and Auntie Joy dancing and exclaiming around them.

It was half an hour before the picnic could really begin. By then Robin was sitting on one of the folding chairs with his foot resting on a cushion on the other chair. This meant that both his parents were sitting on the grass. Robin's foot was bandaged with his father's handkerchief and the blood had soaked right through it and had made a great stain on the yellow cushion. Robin's shorts were hanging over the car bumper where they were dripping on to Nigel's comic, Robin was wearing his swimming trunks and had his mother's new pink cardigan draped round his shoulders. There was blood on that, too.

'*Everyone's* got a bit of blood,' he noted with satisfaction.

Admittedly, his father and Uncle Joe had come off worst. His father sat half on the rug and half off with his trousers dripping. He had to keep squinting about him and twisting his head round to see through the one remaining lens of his glasses. Robin kept staring at him, thinking how strange he looked with one small, squinting eye and one familiar large one behind the thick pebble lens. It made him look a different person—more a creature than a person, really, like something come up from under the sea.

'Are you comfy, dear?' asked his mother.

Robin nodded.

'Are you hungry?'

Robin nodded.

'Ravenous.'

'Pass Robin a sandwich, Nigel!' said Auntie Joy sharply. 'Sitting there pigging yourself! And you'd better not have any more, till we see how many Robin wants. Bless his heart! Does he look pale to you, Myra?'

The picnic got better and better every minute. Robin had at least three times his share of strawberries and Auntie Joy made Nigel give Robin his bag of crisps because she caught him sticking out his tongue at Robin. Nigel went off in a huff and found his comic all over blood and the minute he tried to turn the first page, it tore right across.

'That hanky's nearly soaked,' Robin said, watching Auntie Joy helping herself to the last of the strawberries. 'I've never seen so much blood. You should have seen it dripping into the water. It turned the whole stream a sort of horrible streaky red.'

Auntie Joy carried on spooning.

'If I'd been in the sea, I expect it'd have turned the whole *sea* red,' Robin went on. 'It was the thickest blood I ever saw. Sticky, thicky red blood—streams of it. Gallons. I bet it's killed

Funnybones

all the fishes.'

Auntie Joy gulped and bravely spooned out the remaining juice.

'I won't bleed to death, will I?' he went on. 'Bleed and bleed and bleed till there isn't another drop of blood left in my whole body, and I'm dead. Just like an empty bag, I'd be.'

Auntie Joy turned pale and put down her spoon.

'Just an empty bag of skin,' repeated Robin thoughtfully. 'That's what I'll be.'

'Of course you won't, darling!' cried his mother.

'Well this handkerchief certainly is bloody,' said Robin. 'There must've been a bucket of blood. A *bowlful* anyway!'

Auntie Joy pushed away her bowl of strawberries.

'I wonder what it could've been?' went on Robin. 'That cut me, I mean.'

'Glass!' his mother said. 'It must have been. It's disgraceful, leaving broken glass lying about like that. Someone might have been crippled for life.'

'Dad,' said Robin, after a pause. At first his father did not hear. He had stretched out full length and was peering closely at his newspaper with his one pebble eye.

'Dad!' His father looked up. 'Dad, hadn't you better go and pick *your* glass up? From your specs, I mean? Somebody else might go and cut themselves.'

'The child's right!' his mother cried. 'Fancy the angel thinking of that! Off you go, George, and pick it up, straight away!'

Robin's father got up slowly. His trousers flapped wetly about his legs and his bloodstained shirt clung to him.

'And mind you pick up every little bit!' she called after him. 'Don't you want those strawberries, Joy?'

She shook her head.

'Could you manage them, Robin?'

Robin could. He did. When he had finished, he licked the bowl.

Once the tea things were cleared away, everyone settled down. Auntie Joy was knitting a complicated lacy jacket that meant she had to keep counting under her breath. His mother read, Uncle Joe decided to wash his car, and his father was searching for the sports pages of his newspaper that had

50

blown away while he was down at the beck picking up his broken spectacles. Nigel had a new model yacht and took it down to the stream. Robin watched him go. All *he* had was a sodden comic, and the bugle.

He played the bugle until the back of his father's neck was crimson again and Auntie Joy had twice lost count of her stitches and had to go right back to the beginning of the row again. For a change, he tried letting her get half way across a row and then, without warning, gave a deafening blast. She jumped, the needles jerked, and half the stitches came off.

After the third time, even that didn't seem funny any more. Robin swung his legs down and tested the bad foot. Surprisingly, it hardly hurt at all. He stood right up and took a few steps. His mother looked up.

'Robin!' she squealed. 'Darling! What are you doing?'

'It's all right, Mum,' he said. 'It doesn't hurt. It's stopped bleeding now. It looks worse than it is, the handkerchief being all bloody.'

'I really think you should sit still,' she said.

Robin took no notice and went limping down to the beck. Nigel was in midstream, turning his yacht. It was a beauty.

'Swap you it for my bugle,' he said, after a time.

'What?' Nigel turned to face him. 'You're crazy. Crazy little kid!'

'I'll swap,' repeated Robin.

'Well, I *won't.*' Nigel turned his back again.

Robin stayed where he was. Lying by his feet were Nigel's shoes, with the socks stuffed inside them. Gently, using the big toe of his bandaged foot, he edged them off the bank and into the water. They lay there; the shoes filled and the socks began to balloon and sway. Fascinated, Robin watched. At last the socks, with a final graceful swirl, drifted free of the shoes and began to float downstream.

Robin watched them out of sight. After that, there seemed nothing he could do. What *could* you do, with your foot all bandaged up? The picnic was going all to pieces.

He felt a little sting on his good leg and looked down in time to see a gnat making off. He swatted hard at it, and with a sudden inspiration clapped a hand to his leg, fell to his knees and let out a blood-curdling howl.

'Robin!' He heard his mother scream. 'Robin!'

They were thundering down the slope towards him now, all of them, even Uncle Joe, wash leather in hand.

'Darling! What is it?'

'Snake!' gasped Robin, squeezing his leg tight with his fingers.

'Where?' cried Auntie Joy. He pointed upstream, towards the long grass. He noticed that her wool was wound round her waist and her knitting trailing behind her, both needles missing.

'Where did it *bite* you?' she cried.

Robin took his hands away from the leg. Where they had clutched it, the skin was red and in the the middle of the crimson patch was the tiny bite made by the gnat.

'Oooooh!' He heard his mother give an odd, sighing moan and looked up in time to see that she was falling. His father leapt forward and caught her just in time and they both fell to the ground together.

'Biting the dust,' thought Robin, watching them.

Uncle Joe picked him up for the second time that day and carried him away. Over his shoulder Robin could see the others bending over his mother, trying to lift her. Best of all, he could see Nigel beating round in the long grass with a stick while his boat, forgotten, sailed slowly off downstream.

'Gone,' Robin thought. 'Gone for ever.'

Uncle Joe put him down in the driving seat of his own car.

'Be all right for a minute, old chap?' he asked.

Robin nodded.

'Have a mint.' He fished one from his pocket. 'Back in a minute. Better go and see if I can find that brute of a snake. Don't want Nigel bitten.'

Then he was gone. Robin stared through the window towards the excited huddle by the bank. It seemed to him that everyone was having a good time except himself. There he sat, quite alone, scratching absently at the gnat bite.

Idly he looked about the inside of the car. Usually he wasn't allowed in. It was Uncle Joe's pride and joy. The dashboard glittered with buttons and dials. He pushed one or two of them, and got the radio working, then a green light on, then a red, then the windscreen wipers working. He pushed the gearstick and it slotted smoothly into place. To his left, between the bucket seats, was the handbrake. He knew how to release it—his father had shown him.

The brake was tightly on, and it was a struggle. He was red in the face and panting by the time he sat upright again. The car was rolling forward, very gently, down the grassy slope, then gathering speed as it approached the beck.

By the time they saw him it was too late. The car lurched, then bounced off the bank and into the water. It stopped, right in mid-stream.

Robin looked out and saw himself surrounded by water.

'The captain goes down with his ship!' he thought.

He saw his mother sit up, stare, then fall straight back again. He saw the others, wet, bloodstained and horror-struck, advancing towards him.

With a sigh he let his hands fall from the wheel. It was the end of the picnic, he could see that. He wound down the window and put out a hand to wave. Instead, it met glass and warm flesh. He heard a splash and a tinkle. Level with the window, he saw his father's face. Now *both* his eyes were small and squinting. Small, squinting and murderous.

The picnic was definitely over.

FORREST CARTER

A *Night on the Mountain*

Little Tree was five and an orphan when he went to live in his Cherokee grandparents' Tennessee log cabin. Some years later . . .

Me and Granpa thought Indian. Later people would tell me that this is naive – but I knew – and I remembered what Grampa said about 'words'. If it is 'naive,' it does not matter, for it is also good. Granpa said it would always carry me through . . . which it has; like the time the big-city men made a trip to our mountains.

Granpa was half Scot, but he thought Indian. Such seemed to be the case with others, like the great Red Eagle, Bill Weatherford, or Emperor McGilvery or McIntosh. They gave themselves, as the Indian did, to nature, not trying to subdue it, or pervert it, but to live with it. And so they loved the thought, and loving it grew to be it, so that they could not think as the white man.

Granpa told me. The Indian brought something to trade and laid it at the white man's feet. If he saw nothing he wanted, he picked up his wares and walked off. The white man, not understanding, called him an 'Indian giver' meaning one who gives and then takes back. This is not so. If the Indian gives a gift, he will make no ceremony of it, but will simply leave it to be found.

Granpa said the Indian held his palm up to show 'peace', that he held no weapon. This was logical to Granpa but seemed funny as hell to everybody else. Granpa said the white man meant the same thing by shaking hands, except his words was so crooked, he had to try to shake a weapon out of the sleeve of the feller who claimed he was a friend. Granpa was not given much to handshaking, as he said he didn't like for a man to try to shake something out of his sleeve after he had presented himself as a friend. It was total distrustful of a man's word. Which is reasonable.

As to folks saying, 'How!' and then laughing when they see an Indian, Granpa said it all come about over a couple of hundred years. He said every time the Indian met a white man, the white man commenced to ask him: *how* are you feeling, or *how* are your people, or *how* are you getting along, or *how* is the game where you come from, and so on. He said the Indian come to believe that the white man's favourite subject was *how*; and so, being polite when he met the white man, he figured he would just say *how* and then let the son of a bitch talk about whichever *how* he wanted to. Granpa said people laughing at that was laughing at an Indian who was trying to be courteous and considerate.

We had delivered our wares to the crossroads store and Mr Jenkins said two big-city men had been there. He said they was from Chattanooga and drove a long black automobile. Mr Jenkins said they wanted to talk to Granpa.

Granpa looked at Mr Jenkins from under his big hat. 'Tax-law?'

'No,' Mr Jenkins said. 'They wasn't law at all. Said they was in the whiskey trade. Said they heard tell you was a good maker and they wanted to put you in a big still, and that you could get rich working for them.'

Granpa didn't say anything. He bought some coffee and sugar for Granma. I picked up the wood chips and taken the old candy off Mr Jenkins' hands. Mr Jenkins fidgeted around to hear what Granpa had to say about it, but he knew Granpa too well to ask.

'They said they would be back,' Mr Jenkins said.

Granpa bought some cheese . . . which I was glad, as I like cheese. We walked out, and didn't hang around the store; but headed straight off up the trail. Granpa walked fast. I hadn't time to pick berries and had to do away with the old candy while I was in a continual trot behind Granpa.

When we got to the cabin Granpa told Granma about the big-city men. He said, 'You stay here, Little Tree. I'm going to the still and lay some more covering branches over it. If they come, you let me know.' He taken off, up the hollow trail.

I set on the front porch watching for the big-city men.

Granpa had not hardly gone from sight when I saw them and told Granma. Granma stayed back, standing in the dogtrot, and we watched them coming up the trail and across the foot log.

They had fine clothes like politicians. The big fat man wore a lavender suit and white tie. The skinny man had on a white suit and black shirt which shined. They wore big-city hats made of fine straw.

They walked right up to the porch, though they didn't mount the steps. The big man was sweating pretty bad. He looked at Granma. 'We want to see the old man,' he said. I figured he was sick, for his breathing was bad and it was hard to see his eyes. His eyes looked slitted, way back in swelled-up fat.

Granma didn't say anything. I didn't either. The big man turned around to the skinny man.'The old squaw don't understand English, Slick.'

Mr Slick was looking around over his shoulder, though I didn't see anything behind him. He had a high voice. 'Screw the old squaw,' he said, 'I don't like this place, Chunk—too far back in the mountains. Let's get outa here.' Mr Slick had a little mustache.

'Shut up,' Mr Chunk said. Mr Chunk pushed his hat back. He didn't have any hair. He looked at me setting in the chair.

'The boy looks like a breed,' he said. 'Maybe he understands English. Do you understand English, boy?'

I said, 'I reckin.'

Mr Chunk looked at Mr Slick. 'Hear that . . . he reckins.' They got tickled about this and laughed right loud about it. I saw Granma move back and turn Blue Boy out. He headed up the hollow for Granpa.

Mr Chunk said, 'Where's your Pa, boy?' I told him I didn't recollect my Pa; that I lived here with Granpa and Granma. Mr Chunk wanted to know where Granpa was, and I pointed back up the trail. He reached in his pocket and took out a whole dollar and held it out towards me. 'You can have this dollar, boy, if you take us to your Granpa.'

He had big rings on his fingers. I seen right off that he was rich and more than likely could afford the dollar. I taken it and put it in my pocket. I knew figures pretty well. Even splitting with Granpa, I would get back the fifty cents which I had been slickered out of by the Christian.

I felt pretty good about the whole thing, leading them up the trail. But as we walked I commenced to think. I couldn't take them to the still. I led them up the high trail.

As we walked up the high trail, I felt kind of bad about it, and I didn't have any idea in the world what I was going to do. Mr Chunk and Mr Slick, however, was in fine spirits. They pulled off their coats and walked long behind me. Each one had a pistol in his belt. Mr Slick said, 'Don't remember your Pa, huh kid?' I stopped and said I hadn't no recollection of him at all. Mr Slick said, 'That would make you a bastard, wouldn't it, kid?' I said I reckined, though I had not got to the B's in the dictionary and had not studied that word. They both laughed until they commenced coughing. I laughed too. They seemed like happy fellers.

Mr Chunk said, 'Hell, they're all a bunch of animals.' I said we had lots of animals in the mountains . . . wild-cats and wild hogs; and me and Granpa had seen a black bear oncet.

Mr Slick wanted to know if we had seen one lately. I said we hadn't but we had seen signs. I pointed to a poplar tree where a bear had taken a claw swipe. 'There's sign right there,' I said. Mr Chunk jumped sideways like a snake had struck at him. He bumped into Mr Slick and knocked him down. Mr Slick got mad. 'Goddam you, Chunk, you nearly knocked me off the trail! If you had knocked me down there . . . Mr Slick pointed down into the hollow. Him and Mr Chunk both leaned over and looked down. You could barely see the spring branch, far below us.

'God almighty,' Mr Chunk said, 'how high are we? Hell, if you slipped off this trail, you'd break your neck.' I told Mr Chunk I didn't know how high we was, but I reckined it was pretty high; though I had never give any thought to it.

The higher we got, the more Mr Chunk and Mr Slick coughed. They also fell farther and farther behind me. Once I come back down the trail looking for them, and they were sprawled out under a white oak. The white oak had poison ivy all around its roots. They was laying in the middle of it.

Poison ivy is pretty and green, but you had better not lay in it. It will pop welts out all over you and make sores that will last for months. I didn't say anything about the poison ivy. They was already in it anyway, and I didn't want to make them feel worse about things. They was looking pretty bad.

Mr Slick raised his head up. 'Listen, you little bastard,' he said, 'how much farther we got to go?' Mr Chunk didn't raise his head. He laid there in the poison ivy with his eyes closed. I said we was nearly there.

I had been thinking I knew that Granma would send Granpa up the high trail after me, so when we got to the top of the mountain, I was going to tell Mr Slick and Mr Chunk that we would just set down and wait; that Granpa would be along directly. Which he would. I figured it would work all right and I could keep the dollar, seeing as how I would have, more or less, taken them to Granpa.

I set off up the trail. Mr Slick helped Mr Chunk out of the poison ivy patch and they kind of staggered along behind me. They left their coats in the patch. Mr Chunk said they would get the coats on the way back.

I got to the top of the mountain a long time before they did. The high trail was part of a lot of trails, old Cherokee trails that ran along the rim of the mountain, but forked, going down the mountain on the other side, and forked four or five times on the way down. Granpa said the trails led maybe a hundred miles back into the mountains.

I set down under a bush where the trail made a fork; one branch running the top of the mountain, the other dipping over the mountain down the other side. I figured I would wait on Mr Chunk and Mr Slick, and we would all set here until Granpa come.

It took them a long time. When they finally come over the top of the mountain, Mr Chunk had his arm over Mr Slick's shoulders. He had hurt his foot, more than likely, for he was limping and hopping pretty bad.

Mr Chunk was saying that Mr Slick was a bastard. Which surprised me, as Mr Slick had not said anything about being a bastard too. Mr Chunk was saying that Mr Slick was the one who originally thought up the idea of putting mountain hicks to work for them. Mr Slick said it was Mr Chunk's idea to pick this damn Indian and that Mr Chunk was a son of a bitch.

They was talking so loud, they passed right by me. I didn't have a chance to tell them we had all ought to wait, as Granpa had learnt me not to interrupt when people was talking. They went on down the trail on the other side of the mountain. I watched them until they disappeared amongst the trees, heading into a deep cleft between the mountains. I figured I had better wait on Granpa.

I didn't have to wait long. Blue Boy showed up first. I saw him sniffing my trail, and he come up, tail wagging. In a minute I heard a whippoorwill. It sounded exactly like a whip-poorwill . . . but as it was not dusk dark yet, I knew it was Granpa. I whippoorwilled back, might near as good.

I saw his shadow slipping through the trees in the late evening sun. He wasn't following the trail, and you could never hear him, if he didn't want to be heard. In a minute there he was. I was glad to see him.

I told Granpa that Mr Slick and Mr Chunk had gone on down the trail, and also everything I could remember they said while we was walking. Granpa grunted and didn't say anything, but his eyes narrowed down.

Granma had sent us vittles in a sack, and me and Granpa set down under a cedar and ate. Corn pone and catfish cooked in meal taste good in the air of a high mountain. We finished off all of it.

I showed Granpa the dollar, which I reckined if Mr Chunk figured I had done my job I could keep. I told Granpa soon as we got some change we could split it. Granpa said I had done my job, as he was here to see Mr Chunk. Granpa said I could keep the whole dollar.

I told Granpa about the green and red box at Mr Jenkins' store. I said I figured, more than likely, it wasn't much over a dollar. Granpa said he figured that too. Far off, we heard a yell down in the cleft of the mountain. We had plumb forgot about Mr Chunk and Mr Slick.

It was getting dusk dark. Whippoorwills and chip-wills had started singing on the side of the mountain. Granpa stood up and cupped his hands around his mouth. 'WHOOOOOOOO-

EEEEEEEEEE!' Granpa hollered down the mountain. The sound bounced off another mountain as plain as if Granpa had been over there; then it bounced into the cleft and on up the hollows, getting weaker and weaker. There wasn't any way of figuring where the sound had come from. The echoes had barely died away when we heard three gun shots from down in the cleft. The sound bounced around and travelled off.

'Pistols,' Granpa said. 'They're answering with pistol fire.'

Granpa cut loose again. 'WHOOOOOOEEEEEEEE!' I did too. Which both of us hollering made the echoes jump and bounce even more. The pistol went off again, three times.

Me and Granpa kept hollering. It was fun, listening to the echoes. Each time the pistol answered us, until it didn't answer the last time.

'They're out of bullets,' Granpa said. It was dark now. Granpa stretched and yawned. 'No need me and ye thrashing around down there tonight, Little Tree, trying to git 'em out. They'll be all right. We'll git 'em tomorrow.' Which suited me.

Me and Granpa pulled spring boughs under the cedar tree to sleep on. If you're going to sleep out in the mountains during spring and summer, you had better sleep on spring boughs. If you don't, red bugs will eat you up. Red bugs are so little, you can't hardly see them with the naked eye. They are all over leaves and bushes, by the millions. They will crawl on you and bury up in your skin, causing rashes of bumps to break out all over you. Some years they are worse than others. This was a bad red bug year. There are also wood ticks.

Me and Granpa and Blue Boy crawled up on the spring boughs. Blue Boy curled up by me and felt warm in the sharp air. The boughs were soft and springy. I commenced yawning.

Me and Granpa clasped our hands behind our heads and watched the moon come up. It was full and yellow, slipping over a far mountain. We could see might near a hundred miles, Granpa said, mountains humping and dipping in the moon spray, making shadows and deep purples in their hollows. Fog drifted along in threads, far below us . . . moving through the hollows, snaking around the sides of the mountains. One little patch of fog would come around the end of a mountain like a silver boat and bump into another one and they would melt together and take off up a hollow. Granpa said the fog looked alive. Which it did.

A mockingbird set up song right near us in a high elm. Far back in the mountains, we heard two wild-cats mating. They sounded like they were screaming mad, but Granpa said mating feels so good that cats can't help but scream about it.

I told Granpa I would might near like to sleep on a mountaintop every night. He said he would too. A screech owl screeched down below us, and then there was yells and screams. Granpa said it was Mr Chunk and Mr Slick. He said if they didn't settle down, they would disturb practical all the birds and animals on the mountainside. I went to sleep looking at the moon.

Me and Granpa woke at dawn. There is not anything like dawn from the top of the high mountain. Me and Granpa, and Blue Boy too, watched it. The sky was a light grey, and the birds getting up for the new day made fuss and twitters in the trees.

Away across a hundred miles, the mountaintops humped like islands in the fog that floated below us. Granpa pointed to the east and said, 'Watch.'

Above the rim of the farthest mountain, on the end of the world, a pink streak whipped across, a paintbrush swept a million miles across the sky. Morning wind picked up and hit our faces and me and Granpa knew the colours and the morning birth had come alive. The paintbrush run up in streaks— red, yellow and blue. The mountain rim looked like it had caught fire; then the sun cleared the trees. It turned the fog into a pink ocean, heaving and moving down below.

The sun hit me and Granpa in the face. The world had got born all over again. Granpa said it had, and he taken off his hat and we watched it for a long time. Me and Granpa had a feeling, and I knew right off that we would come again to the mountaintop and watch the morning come.

The sun cleared the mountain and floated free in the sky, and Granpa sighed and stretched. 'Well,' he said, 'ye and me have got work to do. Tell ye what,' Granpa scratched his head, 'tell ye what,' he said again, 'ye trot down to the cabin and tell Granma we'll be up here awhile. Tell her to fix ye and me something to eat and put it in a paper sack, and fix them two big-city fellers something to eat and put it in a tow sack. Can ye remember now—paper sack and tow sack?' I said I could. I started off.

Granpa stopped me. 'And Little Tree,' he said, and commenced grinning about something, 'before Granma fixes the two fellers something to eat, ye tell everything ye can recollect that the two fellers said to ye.' I said I would, and I set off down the trail. Blue Boy went with me. I heard Granpa commence to call up Mr Chunk and Mr Slick. Granpa was yelling, 'WHOOOOOOOOEEEEEEEEE!' I would have liked to stayed and hollered too, but I didn't mind running down the trail, especially early in the morning.

This was the time of morning when all the creatures were coming out for the day living. I saw two 'coons, high in a walnut tree. They peeped down at me and talked as I passed under them. Squirrels chattered and leapt across the trail. They set up and fussed at me as I walked by. Birds dipped and fluttered all along the trail, and a mockingbird followed me and Blue Boy a long way, dipping down at my head, teasing. Mockingbirds will do this if they know you like them. Which I do.

When I got to the cabin clearing, Granma was setting on the back porch. She knew I was coming, I figured, by watching the birds, though I suspicioned that Granma could smell anybody coming, for she was never surprised.

I told her Granpa wanted something to eat in a paper sack for me and him, and for Mr Chunk and Mr Slick, something to be put in a tow sack. Granma commenced to cook up the vittles.

She had fixed mine and Granpa's, and was frying fish for Mr Chunk and Mr Slick, when I recollected to tell her what they had said. While I was telling her, of a sudden she pulled the frying pan off the fire and got out a pot which she filled with water. She dropped Mr Chunk and Mr Slick's fish in the pot. I reckined she had decided to boil their fish instead of frying, but I had never seen her use the root powders, in cooking, that she put in their pot. Their fish got a good boiling.

I told Granma Mr Chunk and Mr Slick 'peared to be good

spirited fellers. I told her that I originally thought we was all laughing because I was a bastard, but it turned out, what they was more than likely laughing at was Mr Slick's being one too, as I had heard Mr Chunk remind him.

Granma put some more root powders in the pot. I told her about the dollar—that Granpa said I had done my job and could keep it. Granma said I could keep it too. She put the dollar in my fruit jar for me but I didn't tell her about the red and green box. There was not any Christians about, as I knew of, but I wasn't going to take any chances.

Granma boiled the fish until the steam got heavy. Her eyes was watering down over her face and she was blowing her nose. She said she reckined it was the steam. Granma put the fish for the big-city fellers in the tow sack and I set off up the high trail. Granma turned all the hounds out, and they went with me.

When I got to the top of the mountain, I didn't see Granpa. I whistled and he answered from halfway down the other side. I went down the trail. It was narrow and shaded over with trees. Granpa said he had practical called up Mr Chunk and Mr Slick out of the cleft. He said they was answering him pretty regular and ought to be coming in sight pretty soon.

Granpa taken their sack of fish and hung it down from a tree limb, right over the trail where they couldn't miss it. Me and Granpa moved back up the trail a ways, and set down under persimmon bushes to eat our dinner. The sun was might near straight up.

Granpa made the dogs lay down, and we eat on our corn pone and fish. Granpa said it had taken him some time to get Mr Chunk and Mr Slick to understanding which direction they was to take towards his voice but they was finally coming. Then we saw them.

If I had not known them right well, I couldn't have recollected as having ever seen them before. Their shirts was tore up complete. They had big cuts and scratches over their arms and faces. Granpa said it looked like they had run through briar patches. Granpa said he couldn't figure how they got all the big red lumps on their faces. I didn't say anything—as it was none of my business—but I figured it was from laying in the poison ivy vines. Mr Chunk had lost a shoe. They come up the trail slow and heads down.

When they saw the tow sack hanging over the trail, they taken it loose from the tree limb and set down. They ate all of Granma's fish, and argued pretty regular over which was getting the most of it. We could hear them plain.

After they finished eating, they stretched out on the trail in the shade. I figured Granpa would go down and get them up, but he didn't. We just set and watched. After a while, Granpa said it was better to let them rest awhile. They didn't rest long.

Mr Chunk jumped up. He was bent over and holding his stomach. He run into the bushes at the side of the trail and pulled his britches down. He squatted and commenced to yell, 'Oh! Goddam! My insides is coming out!' Mr Slick done the same thing. He yelled too. They groaned and hollered and rolled on the ground. In a little while, both of them crawled out of the bushes and laid down on the trail. They didn't lay down long, but jumped up and done it all over again. They taken on so loud that the dogs got excited and Granpa had to quieten them.

I told Granpa it 'peared to me that they was squatting in a poison ivy patch. Granpa said it looked like they was. Also, I told Granpa, they was wiping theirselves with poison ivy leaves. Granpa said more than likely they was. One time, Mr Slick run from the trail back into the poison ivy patch but did not get his britches down in time. He commenced to have some trouble after that with flies buzzing over him. This went on for might near an hour. After that, they laid flat out in the trail, resting up. Granpa said more than likely it was something they had ate which didn't agree with them.

Granpa stepped out in the trail and whistled down to them. Both of them got on their hands and knees and looked up towards me and Granpa. Leastwise, I think they looked at us, but their eyes were swelled might near shut. Both of them yelled.

'Wait a minute,' Mr Chunk hollered. Mr Slick kind of screamed, 'Hold on, man—for God's sake!' They got to their feet and scrambled up the trail. Me and Granpa went on up the trail to the top of the mountain. When we looked back, they was limping behind us.

Granpa said we might as well go back down the trail to the cabin, as they could now find their way out, and would be along d'rectly. So we did.

It was late sun by the time me and Granpa got to the cabin. We set on the back porch with Granma and waited for Mr Chunk and Mr Slick to come along. It was two hours later and dusk dark when they made it to the clearing. Mr Chunk had lost his other shoe and 'peared to tiptoe along.

They made a wide circle around the cabin, which surprised me, as I figured they wanted to see Granpa, but they had changed their minds. I asked Granpa about keeping my dollar. He said I could, as I had done my part of the job. It was not my fault if they changed their minds. Which is reasonable.

I followed them around the cabin. They crossed the foot log and I hollered and waved to them, 'Goodbye, Mr Chunk. Goodbye, Mr Slick. I thankee for the dollar, Mr Chunk.'

Mr Chunk turned and 'peared to shake his fist at me. He fell off the foot log into the spring branch. He grabbed at Mr Slick and nearly pulled him off, but Mr Slick kept his balance and made it across. Mr Slick reminded Mr Chunk that he was a son of a bitch, and Mr Chunk, as he crawled out of the spring branch, said that when he got back to Chattanooga—if he ever did—he was going to kill Mr Slick. Though I don't know why they had fell out with one another.

They passed out of sight down the hollow trail. Granma wanted to send the dogs after them, but Granpa said no. He said he figured they was total wore out.

Granpa said he reckined it all come about from a misunderstanding on Mr Chunk and Mr Slick's part, regarding me and Granpa working for them in the whiskey trade. I figured more than likely it was too.

It had all taken up the best part of two days of mine and Granpa's time. I had, however, come out a dollar ahead. I cautioned Granpa that I was still willing and stood ready to split the dollar with him as we was partners, but he said no, I had earned the dollar without any connection in the whiskey trade. Granpa said all things considered it was not bad pay for the work. Which it wasn't.

Our Solar System

We made a model of the Solar System today
On our school field after lunch.
Sir chose nine of us
To be planets
And he parked the rest of the class
In the middle of the field
In a thoroughly messy bunch.
'You're the sun,' he brays,
'Big, huge; stick your arms out
In all directions
To show the sun's rays.'
The bit about sticking arms out
Really wasn't very wise
And I don't mind telling you
A few fingers and elbows
Got stuck in a few eyes.
Big Bill took a poke at Tony
And only narrowly missed him,
And altogether it looked
More like a shambles
Than the start of the Solar System.
The nine of us who were planets
Didn't get a lot of fun:
I was Mercury and I stood
Like a Charlie
Nearest of all to the sun,
And all the sun crowd
Blew raspberries and shouted,
'This is the one we'll roast!
We're going to scorch you up, Titch,
You'll be like a black slice of toast!'
Katy was Venus and Val was Earth
And Neville Stephens was Mars,
And the sun kids shouted and
Wanted to know

Could he spare them any of his Bars.
A big gap then to Jupiter (Jayne)
And a bigger one still to Saturn,
And Sir's excited and rambling on
About the System's mighty pattern.
'Now, a walloping space to Uranus,' he bawls,
'It's quite a bike ride away from the sun.'
Ha blooming ha – at least somebody here's
Having a load of fun.
He's got two planet kids left
And Karen's moaning
About having to walk so far:
She's Neptune – I suppose Sir's
Cracking some joke about
Doing X million miles by car.
Pete's Pluto—'The farthest flung of all,'
Says Sir,
He's put by the hedge and rests,
But soon he starts picking blackberries
And poking at old birds' nests.
'Of course,' yells Sir, 'the scale's not right
But it'll give you
A rough idea.
Now, when I blow my whistle
I want you all to start on your orbits –
Clear?'
Well, it wasn't of course,
And most of the class, well,
Their hearts weren't really in it,
Still, Sir's O.K. so we gave it a go,
With me popping round the sun
About ten times a minute,
And Pluto on the hedge ambling round
Fit to finish his orbit next year.
We'd still have been there but

A kid came out of the school and yelled,
'The bell's gone and the school bus's here!'
Well, the Solar System
Broke up pretty fast,
And my bus money had gone from my sock
And I had to borrow.
I suppose we'll have to draw diagrams
And write about it tomorrow.

Eric Finney

Dead Thick

No. I haven't kept up with the modern stuff.
Haven't read a book in years.
Textbooks? A few, but nothing new.
Mind you, it's not that I don't
Have the inclination, just that
Nothing's grabbed my fancy.

Still, I like what I've read: Hardy,
Golding, I'll flick through
Graham Greene if I have to.
But no, nothing new. Mind you
I read the reviews. They contain
A lot of sharp observation.
After reading a couple I find
I can form my own opinion.

I'm too busy for literature, that's the problem.
I'm after promotion. Ideally what I'd like
Is a job in administration.
What do I do? Teach. English.
It's exhausting. The kids are thick.
They've nothing between their ears.
Do you know what? Some of them
Haven't read a book in years.

Brian Patten

An Essay Justifying the Place of Science in the School Curriculum

Our physics teacher's Skullhead,
he's dead thin,
but has some dead good textbooks
with cartoons
where little men drop things
off blocks of flats.

Gravity is what
we did last week.

This morning Mrs Simpson
told me off
for having laddered tights
and said I must
appreciate the gravity
of crime.

Next week we're doing friction.
My mum thinks
that there is too much friction
in this world.

Chemistry we have
with Basher Bates.
We sit around his desk
while he does things
to litmus paper, it
goes red and green,
or is that colour blindness.

Well, this year
we have to choose our options
and I'd like
to do physics because

of the cartoons,
but can't because of chemistry
with Bates –
I'd have to take that too
you see, and Bates
once sent me out of class
because I laughed,
and laughing's not allowed
in chemistry.

Jayne Hollinson

MARIA MORRIS

T houghts on Paper

Well, there I was, stamping the name of our school onto the fly-leaves of a whole batch of books and what did I come across? A spanking new pile of crispy white paper, that's what. Actually, it wasn't really spanking new, in fact, judging by the layer of dust which buried it and the dejected way in which it sat in one corner of that jungle of a stockroom, I'd say it had been there a good few years. Well, being kind-hearted, I decided to take this lonely wad of whiteness into my care . . . and here it is, receiving the attention of my pen, but enough about that.

I've decided to dedicate my wild and crazy teenage thoughts to this loyal paper, so that I've got something to do while Mum and Dad are downstairs having a screaming match. I think *he's* come back to collect the rest of his possessions, the ones he forgot to take with him last time he was round, and the time before and the time before that. I'd have thought he'd have got the message by now; Mum doesn't want him and neither do I. It's his own fault though, he brought it upon himself, I mean, would you be very happy with a dad who went and 'got acquainted' with another woman? And to think, he promised to love and cherish Mum, 'till death do us part'. But then all males of any description are the same, it's just that Dad went too far; he was always spending his money on things other than his family.

Some of my mates reckon that boys are the best things since sliced bread, whereas I tend to think of them as a bunch of showground poodles, with their permed hair and trendy Nike trainers, along with their personalised six-foot ghetto blasters.

Parents. Are they all like mine, or am I the only individual on the whole of this globe who has to suffer with parents that I don't understand? Why do they have to quarrel all the time, and over such trivial things too? When they were still together, they used to quibble over things like when they were going to

72

go out, and where they should go, and 'What's wrong with having chips every other day?' (That would be my Dad, by the way.) Another thing that gets me about parents is that when they do finally decide where to go for our holiday, for example, it's usually somewhere like a fortnight in the Lake District, so there we are wandering though boggy marshland in the pouring rain, with nothing but miles and miles of 'beautiful' scenery to look at and the odd blank-faced sheep. I reckon that sheep aren't really that dumb, but the looks on their faces are really those of deep concentration, in fact they're probably thinking complicated philosophical thoughts like 'what is the algebraic equation of the percentage increase of Australian rainfall?' Or, 'what the hell are those fools doing, in boggy marshland in the pouring rain?'

I think I just heard the door slam. He's gone now, for good I hope. I bet you any money that at this very minute, Mum's sitting in the kitchen smoking cigarette after cigarette, without the slightest care in the world about what she's doing to her heart and lungs; but then her heart's ruined now anyway, it'll never repair.

I had a boyfriend once, you know, Never again. After him I wouldn't trust any male, even if he got down on one knee and thrust a bunch of rare and exotic orchids into my arms, knowing the likes of them round here, they'd probably be those plastic ones that squirt water at you through a little hole. I remember seeing a boy do that to his girlfriend once. He got down on one knee just like I said, sang a little verse, then held out these flowers to her and just as she was about to take them, he pressed a little round plastic thing and a jet of water flew out of the fair blossom and was she surprised! She flung her arms up in the air and went beserk: 'Scream, scream, scream!' she went! The end of another happy relationship. My boyfriend wasn't like that, though, I was lucky in that respect. No, my boyfriend was completely different. He was worse. It was good while it lasted though, I've got to admit. Those kisses, wow, those lip-smacking beauties were winners with me every time. I wonder what those other girls thought of his kisses? He must have had a full-time job on his hands, so that's why I decided to make life a little easier for the poor, poor dear.

To be frank, I ditched the two-timing sod.

Exams bother me. Some people like my mate Jill revise till they're blue in the face . . . and pass. Others, like Cyrenna, for example, don't . . . and pass. I do both . . . and fail. I do one . . . and fail. I do the other . . . and fail. What really gets me, is that no matter how hard I slog my guts out for my mum, she ends up going to the school. When my mum goes to the school, it bothers me. Hyperactive parents are always up to something.

I had a French exam yesterday. I sat there for the whole hour doodling on the corner of my desk and reading the etchings. One said, 'Here fell Jo Whitey, murdered by a computing paper no. one. 21/6/84'; another said, 'Sex is evil, evil is sin. Sin is forgotten so . . .' I couldn't read the rest of that one as it was a bit worn away. Shame. 'Pink Floyd' was intricately carved into the wood at one end of the desk, so I decided to add my own little doodle, to bring things up to date. With my compass, I scratched a bumble bee (which happens to be my personal mark), that is until my compass bust; then, just as I was trying to fix it, a teacher came up and looked right down his nose at me. He gave me one of those warning looks that are supposed to scare you, then walked away. I hate French though, and I hate those silly questions they give you in exams. It's all very well asking what direction the loo is, but when it comes to having an interesting conversation with a foreigner, you only ever get as far as talking about the state of the weather lately and can you have a croissant with plenty of mustard please? Then when I reach section B, question two, it turns out to be something like, 'Que fais-tu, Marie-Claude?' Who cares what she's doing, because I know I don't! She could be doing triple-back somersaults and I wouldn't bat an eyelid.

Usually, in lessons such as maths, I give up listening and practise the art of sleeping with my eyes open, which is pretty clever, if you can do it without the teacher jolting you back to consciousness; then you just have to fall on his mercy. 'You weren't paying attention, were you? No? I thought so. One day you'll regret it.' (I think I am already.) 'You'll be sorry, blah blah blah . . .' Then, by the time he's finished you've gone and nodded off again. But the trouble with teachers is that they reckon we're a bunch of thickies who are blind to the world. Only we know what is really going on though. To them, unemployment is a lack of jobs, while to us it is living on a few pounds' dole money, whether we have three 'A' levels in our pockets or not. To them, politics are the complicated rules, ways in which we must live and the matters of society that must be looked into, for the well-being of our country. To us, it is the garble that has made our life what it is today. It isn't The Teacher and The Pupil, or The Elders and Youth, it is Them v. Us.

Once, we had a really soft teacher, I think her name was Miss Brown or something. I remember that she was quite old, the strictly disciplined type, yet when it came to controlling a class of fifteen year olds, she turned into a dithering heap. For a start, Danny Pierce, like the childish fool he is, kept yelling out that he wanted to go for a pee, (you'd have thought he was toilet -trained by now) and then there were the boys at the back, who kept making weird noises, like faulty foghorns and sheep farting. (Why do I keep bringing sheep into this? Do sheep fart?) Well, after Danny had yelled, 'Wee wee!' for about the millionth time, the fire alarm went off. The whole class jumped up at the same time as chairs went flying everywhere and there was a mad rush of hysteria and people scrambling and climbing over each other to get to the door first. Meanwhile, Miss Brown was screeching, 'Naow children,' (she talked like that, did Miss Brown). 'Naow children, we must keep order and contain ourselves. We shall disperse quietly.' Then Danny said, or rather shouted, 'I think I already have!' Anyway, by the time most of us had reached the field for register callings, Miss Brown was still waving her arms about and going, 'Screech screech!' Any other teacher would have bellowed something like, 'Get a move on, you pack o' blinking morons!' It all turned out to be a false alarm in the end, because some jerk smashed the glass on one of those little red boxes (you know the type I mean) by accident, when he slung his bag over his shoulder. It annoys me when they do that, because if you're standing behind them at the time, you end up flat out on the floor, having received a left-hook from a Slazenger bag. Mostly the owner of the vicious bag doesn't even notice what's happened!

My pen's running out, not much left on the ol' clock. I need to buy one. I need cash. I need a job, a part-time job. The thing is, most jobs for people in school are pretty long hours, with small pay, like a newspaper round for example. Every morning you rub your bleary eyes and set off into the rising sun, brave the blizzards, the gales, the torrential downpours. You pole-vault over gates that won't open, fight with fierce dogs and battle with vicious letter boxes. Then when the morning lies are delivered you return to base, mission accomplished, to receive your reward; five old and grubby notes (and in case you're wondering, they're not tenners). That's it in a nutshell really. If however, you want to sweep the floor and lug all the heavy boxes around in a shop, then fine. If you've got a mathematical brain and are not the sort who gives three-quid change from a fifty-pence piece, then I'm sure you'll go far on a till. Or maybe you could work in a pub, pulling pints and picking up the peanuts off the floor, that is if you can bear holding conversations on fly-fishing, listening to people's views on the present figures in the stock exchange and ignoring the sideways glances to certain parts of your anatomy from a group of shifty-looking old men. But enough about jobs. The subject's simply too depressing.

Have any of you fellow girls out there noticed how hard it is to please other people? We're always expected to have twenty-two inch waists which leads to the problem of food. You starve yourself to skin and bone or live on a diet of muesli and carrot juice, you can choose from the wide variety of healthy foods. Picture the scene: you shift your weight (all fourteen stone of it) back and forth along the shelves. Will you have the cardboard flakes (bran crisps), bath sponge sprinkled with scouring powder (lowfat cake with special diet sugar), or will it be a few slices of granite rock, with axle-grease (crispy wholemeal bread with extra healthy margarine)? You're spoilt for choice so buy a Mars bar instead. If you ever manage to obtain the waistline desired, then you are faced with the problem of what type of clothes you should wear. A Littlewood's number bought in the sale is no good, I'm afraid. The main rules are, that they must have a designer label; this is one of the essential ingredients—Lacoste or some other nifty label like Benetton or Pepe. Failing that, you could always pop down to the local jumble sale, which is one of the really hip places to go. But honestly, I remember when if you wore something from a jumble sale, you'd be the laughing stock of the neighbourhood; if you decided to hit the town with whatever number you bought, you'd find that your friends suddenly didn't want to know you: 'Who's she?'

'It's me, your bestest ever pal!'

'Ha ha, very funny. Look, if you don't beat it then you'll be in trouble.'

'B . . . b . . . but . . .'

'You heard, now hop it, and take your purple flares with you.'

Sad isn't it? These days it's all cardigans on your head (worn as a supposedly very trendy hat), leggings round your neck and shoes on your hands. Ah well, that's life.

My pen's nearly died now, so I'll wrap a pair of leggings round my neck, have a quick swig of the ol' carrot juice and see if the sheep in the Lake District can tell me where I can find a job.

ALAN BLEASDALE

Southward Bound

Scully is a fifteen-year-old Liverpudlian whose mates include Mad Dog (because he is one), Half a Dog (because part of his nose is missing) and Mooey. They are trying to hitch to Southampton for a football match.

It was about six o'clock when we got our first lift. It was off a lorry going to Manchester and the driver was a talker. They usually are. That's the real reason most people give lifts, if you want to know. Not to do you a favour, but to tell you about themselves, to tell you what great blokes they are, and what a great life they have. You have to sit there and listen to them and chat them up a bit. It doesn't half make you sick. I just get them started and then let them get on with it.

This driver got all carried away telling us about when he was in Korea and he was in the Marines, and they had to teach the Yanks how to kill proper, because they kept stabbing themselves in the dark. He told us how a mate of his blew all the fingers off his left hand to get out of the fighting, and the roof fell in on him in the hospital and killed him. He got so excited, his lorry started weaving all over the road, and he didn't want to let us out at Haydock.

'I'll take you to the M62. It's better there.'

'No it isn't,' I said. 'I've worked it out.'

We almost had to fight our way out of his cab. He was still talking away as he pulled back onto the road. Have you ever noticed how people from Manchester never stop talking?

There was nobody else waiting at the side of the approach road to the M6. Sometimes, if it's summer or Liverpool are playing Stoke or Wolves or Coventry, you can't get near the Motorway for students or red scarves. We went and stood in the light under the sign that tells you what you can't do on the Motorway.

We were just eating the last of the butties that me Mam had

made me, when the Law arrived in one of them flashy orange and white sports cars. As they pulled in to the hard shoulder where we was standing, they went right through the puddles of rain and splashed us all. All over me corned beef crust it went. Funny sense of humour, the Law. One of the coppers got out and took a couple of deep breaths, as if he was out for a walk in the park. He had a ciggie cupped in his hand behind his back.

'What are you doing?' he said.

You know what, that's just about the worst thing about coppers. They ask you really stupid questions like that one, and then they give you a working over if you tell them you're waiting for a Jumbo Jet to land, or something like that. I mean, what did he think we were doing? Queuing for the Birkenhead Ferry? They must get taught them questions to ask when they're learning how to be coppers. Whoever teaches them should come and stand with us for a bit and listen to them.

'We're waiting for a mate of me dad's,' I said.

'He should be along in a bit,' Mad Dog said.

'You look like you might be hitchin',' he said.

'We're not though,' I said.

'How do I know?'

'I dunno,' I said. 'How do yer know?' Sometimes you can only stand so much. He screwed his face up all tight. His forehead nearly fell over his nose. 'Are you being cheeky, lad?' he said. Another smart question. His brain must have been on time and a half.

'What? Who me?' I said. I looked all shocked and hurt and turned around to see if there was anyone behind me, giving cheek. But there wasn't.

'I can run you all off here, you know. You're not supposed t'be standing here. It's not allowed. It's against the law. You're breakin' the law. Did y'know that?'

'No, we didn't, honest. We've never done anything like this before. Only we're waiting for this feller. This mate of me dad's.'

'So y'keep tellin' me. Where's he comin' from then, this feller, this big mate of your dad's?'

Course, I spotted that as a trick question, straight off. I don't stand there in the pissing down rain thinking of nothing, you know. The others might do, but all the time, while we're waiting, I'm planning things, waiting for the next move. I could spot this copper's angle before he'd even started. If this feller was coming from Liverpool, we wouldn't be standing here at Haydock waiting for him, would we?

'From Manchester,' I said. 'He's a lorry driver. He used to fight in Korea. He was a Marine.' I don't know what made me say that last bit. Straight away, I wished I hadn't.

'An' he's got four fingers shot off his left hand,' Mooey piped up. 'He did it himself, before the roof fell in.'

I thought he was certain to chase us then, but he wasn't really bothered. He'd had enough fresh air. He even laughed at Mooey as he threw his ciggie away.

'If y'still here in twenty minutes, I'll run yer off.'

'Y'won't have to, Mister,' Mooey said, "cos if we're still here then, we'll have gone already, 'cos we're soaked to the skin. Look,' he said, 'I'm only in me pumps.'

We all looked down at his feet. He lifted one leg up and hopped around. All the whitening ran off his pumps, and there was a little patch of white where he'd been standing.

You've got to hand it to Mooey sometimes. You never know whether he's putting it on or not, but there's times when he's more than all there, he's one step ahead. You could see he'd made this copper happy. He could hardly keep a straight face. He couldn't get back to the car fast enough to tell his mate what this loony had just said to him.

'Well, good luck, lads,' he said as he got his fat feet back into the car. 'Don't forget, twenty minutes.'

The law hadn't long gone when two blokes in a big Zodiac came past and stopped about thirty yards ahead of us. We started running up the hill towards them. As we were running, they were looking around at us and laughing. I knew then what they were going to do. I think we all did, except Mooey. It's the only thing that can get me down when I'm thumbin'. It's a really dirty trick. Just before we got to their back bumper, the driver beeped his horn, and they shot off, up the approach road. Fellers like that, they want their gear levers cut off.

Mad Dog went running after them, screaming. 'I'll kill yer, y'bastards, I'll kill yer, I'll kill yer.' He should have had four fingers missing and been carrying a hand grenade. He followed them right off the road onto the Motorway. When he came back, he was frothing at the mouth. I hadn't seen him like that for weeks. Not since his baby sister Teresa peed on his packet of fags coming back from the shops at Eastbank. He had hold of her and she did a fountain right into his jacket pocket. The filters just fell apart.

'8978 AR,' he said to Mooey. 'Remember that for me. 8978 AR.'

'8978AR8978AR8978AR8978AR8978AR. . .'

After about two minutes of that we'd learned it off by heart, and so we let him stop. I counted up to ten and then said, 'Aye Moo, what were those numbers again?'

'What numbers?' he said.

Needless to say, the coppers never came back. Nobody came. It was as if the road was blocked. I'd never seen anything like it for a Friday night. We must have waited well over an hour, and in that time only about a dozen cars and a couple of lorries came past. We was all pig-sick and soaked. I could tell the other wanted to go home but they wouldn't say so.

It was a little green laundry van that stopped in the end. It had 'Lavender Laundries' written on it on the side. Only Mooey had thumbed it, we were so fed up, and anyway, it looked as though it would make it to the next turn-off for Warrington, and then surrender and die. It didn't so much stop as collapse. The feller was walking towards us and the engine was still groaning. He had a torch with him and he flashed it as us.

'What's the matter?' Half A Dog said.

The feller never said anything, but just switched his torch off and started back towards his van.

'Hey,' I said, 'What're y'doin'?' He just kept on walking. 'Y' can't leave us now. Y'stopped.'

'It's not you I'm looking for,' he said. He turned around and plodded back to his van. We ran up to him as he was climbing in. I had to stop Mad Dog getting a grip of him.

'Aren't y'goin' t'give us a lift after all?' I said.

'A lift?' he said. By the look on his face, I think he thought we was talking about elevators. 'Second Floor, Men Shoes and Furniture.'

'That's right. A lift down the Motorway.'

'Sorry,' he said, 'I don't give lifts.'

'But y'stopped. Don't y'remember. Just before. That's why y'out in the rain now.'

'I only wanted to see your faces,' he said.

'What for? Is it y'hobby?'

'I'm lookin' for someone.'

'Who then?'

'My son.'

Jeez, I thought he was going to cry on me shoulder. I wasn't far off meself. I was desperate for that lift. I could see us going home, our Tony calling me a failure, our Arthur laughing at me, me Mam taking me last quid off me.

'A lad about the same age as us?' I said.

'That's right,' he said. For the first time, he showed a bit of life. He had a good look at me. 'A bit older,' he said. 'Bigger.'

'Did he have anythin' with him? Like a bag or a holdall?'

'No, nothing. Just the clothes he was walking around in. He even left his Post Office Saving Book. Seventeen pound he had in there. I reckon she must have had money.' He climbed back into his van.

'There was a girl with him?'

'A woman.'

'Well, that settles it then, mister. We've seen him, there's no doubt about it. In fact, y'only just missed them. Didn't he, lads?'

They all looked at me with their mouths open. I stood up a bit so the feller couldn't see me face, and mouthed 'yes' and nodded me head up and down.

'Yes, that's right, mister,' Mad Dog and Half A Dog said, and Mooey started going, '8978AR8978AR8978AR8978AR. . .' till Half A Dog stood on his pumps.

'If y'd only been here ten minutes ago, y'd have had them. Two blokes in a red Zodiac give them a lift. We were glad to get rid of them too, I can tell yer. It gives us a chance then. I'd be able t'spot them for yer any day. I bet they've stopped at a Motorway Café. If y'take us with yer, we can help y'look. We know all the places.'

'I don't know whether I've got the room,' he said, but by that time we were already at the other door and climbing in.

The van staggered off. Every time it did over forty, his oil light went on and off like an indicator. I was in the front seat. The others let me sit there because they think I like chatting the drivers up. I hate it really. I just like sitting in the front seat.

'Where d'y'come from, mister?' I said.

'Swarthmoor.'

'Hey? Never heard of it.'

'It's near Ulverston.'

'Never heard of that neither,' I said. I was trying to keep him talking so that I could stop, but he wasn't the usual type of bloke what gives us lifts. It was hard work even trying to get him started. 'Is it near anywhere else?' I said after a bit.

'It's between Morecambe and Barrow,' he said about five minutes later.

'I've been to Morecambe,' Half A Dog said from the back. 'For the day, once. I'll never go again. It's not as good as Blackpool. The fair's crap, and that ship they've got by the Pier, it's fallin' apart.'

'Barrow were in the Fourth Division,' I said. 'They were near the bottom, but they got the boot when Hereford came in.'

He just nodded and said, 'that's right,' and kept on driving. He didn't say any more. His windscreen wipers were useless. They kept missing the window, and he had to slow down even more. The speed he was going, we'd have got to Southampton about Wednesday afternoon if we'd stayed with him.

'What were y'doin' at the Haydock turn-off?' I asked him after about half an hour and two miles of silence. 'You was comin' from Manchester.'

'One of Barry's friends told me that they'd talked about getting a job at a café together. I'd just been to the 'Little Chef' on the Bolton Road.'

'No luck then?'

'No,' he said and then he stopped for a bit and sniffed up. 'People just laugh when I tell them,' he said. He was all hunched over his wheel as though it was foggy.

'Well, I seen them, mate,' I said. 'She looked a well-stacked piece too.' As soon as I said it, I wished I hadn't, again. I always get carried away. She could have been a thin midget for all I knew. But he didn't seem to care what I said.

'How old was she?' I said.

'Twenty-six.'

'How old?'

'Twenty-six. Or seven.'

'How old's y'lad then?'

'He was sixteen two weeks ago.'

'Jeezus.'

'And she's married.'

'Christ Almighty.'

'With three kids.'

We all laughed like he said we would.

'How did he meet her?' I said.

'She worked in the chip shop by Ulverston Grammar School.'

'Did he go to the Grammar School?'

'He's taking his "O" Levels next year.'

'He should have stayed School Dinners, mate,' I said.

We had murder at the first Motorway Café getting him to go down to the next one at Keele.

'It's no use,' he said when we got back to his van after we'd searched everywhere except the women's bogs—though Mooey did offer to go in there, even though he had no idea what we were looking for.

I tried to buck him up. 'Y'know, the more I think about it, the more certain I am that they'll be at Keele. It's the best place for gettin' lifts off the lorries y'know. That's where they'll be. They'll be at Keele, fryin' chips in the Transport or trying t'get a lift South.'

He looked at his watch.

'It's not far to Keele, mate. It's only down the road.'

'I promised Ruby I'd be back by midnight.'

'How far back is it t'where y'live?' I asked him.

'It must be over a hundred miles by now,' he said.

'Y'll make it back easy before midnight. There's no traffic on the roads. Y'll bomb along, no messin'. I mean, what would y'feel like if y'went home now, tonight, an' months from now, y'found out that y'lad had been at Keele all the time, on a petrol pump, or repairin' the slot machine or somethin' like that. Ruby'd go mad. She'd blame you straight off for not goin' down there now. Never mind midnight. Y're not Cinderella.'

'I suppose so,' he said. What a misery hole. No wonder his lad legged it. When he got home, he'd probably find that Ruby had took her chance and done a bunk too.

The further South we got, the more traffic there was. At Keele there was loads of cars in the car park, and lorries too, further down. When we got out of the van Mad Dog walked off down the car park, same as he'd done at the other service station at Knutsford.

'Well, thanks, Mister,' I said. 'We'll be off now.'

'Are you going?' he said. 'I thought you might help me look.'

'We're in a bit of a hurry,' I said. 'Anyway, y're bound to find him here.'

'I hope so,' he said.

'Look, is that him, there, in the little cap, by the steps with a brush?'

'No.'

'Oh. Well, anyway, mister, be seein' yer.'

He went to the steps by the Transport Café. Him and his van made a good pair. I could have been there and back twice, and been served, before he got to the doors. He stood outside with his torch in his hand.

'D'y'think he'll find him?' Half A Dog said.

'Nah. No chance,' I said. 'It's like lookin' for bird shit in a cuckoo clock. He won't find him.'

'Ih . . .Ih . . .Ih. . .' Mad Dog said behind us. As I turned around, he grabbed hold of me by me jacket and started shaking me. He had a real tight grip on me as well. It was daft. He was throwing me around because *he* couldn't get his words out. He had another go. 'Ih . . .Ih . . .Ih . . .'

'Hey, steady on there,' I said. 'Watch the old wool and mohair.'

Half A Dog got hold of his wrists and dragged him off me.

He pushed him against the side of the van and grabbed him by the arms and held him tight. Mad Dog calmed down a bit then, but he still couldn't get his words out, and when Half A Dog let him go, he ran down the line of parked cars. We followed him.

He stood next to the back of the Zodiac like as though he was Columbus with America.

'Ih . . .Ih . . .it's h here. Look, eh . . . eh . . . 8978AR. Them bbastards at Heh . . . Heh . . . Hay . . . the Motorway.'

We just stood there for a bit, looking at it as if it was in a shop window.

'Let's rip its tyres off,' Mad Dog said, 'an scratch the peh . . . peh . . . paint, an' break the windows, an' ...'

'An' let's make our getaway in a fast laundry van,' I said. 'Don't be daft, Mad Dog,. If they come out of the café in ten minutes an' find a wreck where their car used t'be, who are they goin' t'blame? Who are the coppers goin' t'pick on first?'

'The four good lookin' lads thumbin' over by the petrol pumps,' Half A Dog said.

'Dead right,' I said.

'So? Wha' are we goin' t'do? Nothin'?' Mad Dog was starting to fidget again.

'Course not,' I said. 'Mooey, come here.'

He came and stood by me.

'Now, this shouldn't take very long, Mooey, y've been in good form lately. All I want y't'do is to think of water. A lot of water, Mooey, not just a little cup full. I want y'to think of the Mersey of a Sunday afternoon, all the boats goin' up an' down, all the water splashin' all over the bottom deck of the Birkenhead ferry, soakin' us, makin' us wet. Wet, Moo. Wet with water. Come on, what's the matter with you? An' what about that time, years ago, at the lake in Dovecot Park before they filled it in, where we used t'go catchin' tiddlers, an' that big lad made y'fill y'fish can full of water, an' drink it all down. And then he made y'thank him for a nice cup of tea, but all the time, deep inside, in y'heart, y'knew it wasn't tea that y'd drunk, it was lake water full of cack an' tiddlers. An' what about that day in Wales when we took y't'see that waterfall, with all the water runnin' an' bouncin' off the rocks, an' the noise of it, glugg, glugg, gluggin' down into the stream at the bottom, just like the noise of the glass of lemonade y'had at the café in the Coach Station, waitin' t'go home. D'y' remember that, Moo, a long cool glass of dandelion an' burdock, drinkin' it all down, all cold an' icy an' wet, inside yer, glugg, glugg, glu . . .'

'Stop it,' he said, as he crossed his legs and bent double. 'Y' makin' me wet meself.' He started hobbling about.

I took the petrol cap off the Zodiac.

'Here, Mooey,' I said. 'Do it in here.'

There was a full tank when we'd all had a go. Mooey took hours. He must have been saving it up, like the other night.

'Hey,' he said as we were walking down past the petrol pumps and onto the approach road onto the Motorway, 'hey, it wasn't me what had t'drink the pond water, y'know. It was Ryan. It was me what he made eat a Brylcreem butty.'

'That's right,' I said. 'Of course. I wondered why y'took so long before y'wanted t'go. I remember now. His name was Johnny Thacker. I gave him two bob not to touch me. As soon as I give it to him, he set their dog on me. Bloody big thing it was, a boxer. I ended up in some woman's house in Gordon Drive.'

'What happened to him?' Mad Dog said.

'He went in the Police,' I said. 'I saw him down the Town with a ten-foot Alsatian, when the Arsenal supporters were on the march after the match last month.'

'It wasn't only that,' Mooey said.

'What?'

'That stopped me weein',' Mooey said. 'I was frightened as well.'

'What of?'

'Of weein' on someone, like I did in your alleyway. I've had bad dreams about that since. I can't wee proper no more neither. It takes ages t'come.'

We were stood under the sign the same as the one at Haydock, that tells you all the things you can't do. They're all exactly the same. We could have had a lift off a petrol tanker as soon as we got there, but the feller was only going to Stoke, and short lifts, now we were on the Motorway, were no good.

We were waiting for the big one. A couple of hundred miles, that's what we wanted.

When we saw the laundry van coming down the approach road, we all stared up at the sky and tried to look as though it wasn't our fault his son wasn't there. When the van stopped and the feller jumped out and came bombing over towards us, I thought for a second he was going to bop me one for lying to him, but as I moved back and banged me head against the sign post, he grabbed hold of me hand and started shaking it, just like as if I was famous, or he was. He nearly took the hand off me. The Prime Minister came to our school once, when I was in the first year, to listen to some singing, and at the end he came around shaking our hands, just like that. And then he tapped his pipe out on me head.

'Wha've I done?' I said. 'What's the matter? Are y'feelin alright?'

'I want to thank you,' he said and he stuck a pound note in the top pocket of me jacket.

'What's this for?'

'Because I've found him,' he said. We all looked over to the car.

Sure enough, there was a lad sitting there with his head down. He was wearing one of them jackets with a hood and all fur around the edges. I could hardly believe it.

'Are y'sure it's him?' I said.

I went over and had a look for meself. He had curly hair and pimples and he was crying. I couldn't see his face proper, he wouldn't look at me.

'Where was he?'

'On the salads in the Restaurant.'

'What's the matter with him?'

'She's left him. Ran off with a traveller in cosmetics yesterday.'

'The woman in the chippie by our house used to be the same. Ran off with a bin-man in the end. It's handlin' all the fish that does it. He's best off without her.'

'That's what I told him.'

He got back in his van and I went around the other side again and give the lad a grin. I even knocked on the window, but his chin was on his tits.

'Give our love to Ruby,' I said as the van crawled off.

'What was that y'was sayin' about a cuckoo clock?' Half A Dog said.

I held up the pound note. 'It's just laid an egg,' I said.

We got fed up hanging around there before long. It was useless. As we were walking back up towards the Service Station, the blokes in the Zodiac came down towards us. They had two birds with them. They must have picked them up in the Transport. There's always birds waiting for lifts in there. They go with the lorry drivers usually. In about half an hour, they'll have wished they had.

'Well,' I said as we stood outside the Transport Cafe, 'if we don't get a move on soon, we've had it. We'll never make it.'

The others didn't say anything but I could tell they was brassed off. The trouble is, they expect chauffeur-driven lorries. 'Southampton, James.' It's not on, that. You've got to rough it a bit.

'The best thing t'do is t'get somethin' t'eat,' I said, 'an' then have one last go. It won't be so bad when we've had a cup of tea an' a chip butty. I'll treat yer out of this quid that the feller give me.'

We was starving. When you're thumbin' you forget about eating, or else you don't get the chance. The only trouble was, we poured sugar on our egg and chips. We thought it was salt. You couldn't tell. It looked just like a big salt cellar. Someone should complain.

We were by the chocolate machine underneath the clock. I'd just come back from the bogs. They're like palaces, them bogs on the Motorway, aren't they?

'Well, it's twenty to twelve,' I said. 'If we haven't got a lift by half past twelve, we'll go home. Okay?'

No answer, so I knocked again. I knew there must be somebody there.

'Are y'all goin' deaf?' I said. 'Is that alright? Are we agreed on that?'

'Er well er . . . Scull . . . er no hard feelin's, like,' Half A Dog said, 'but er . . . when y' was in the er . . . bog, we had a little like er talk, an' er . . . it turns out like that er most of us . . . '

He looked around at the other two, but Mad Dog was pretending he wasn't there, and Mooey wasn't, so he carried on alone. 'An well er we . . . think we er should . . . er go home . . . er sooner. Like right now . . . er like.'

'If that's what y'want, y'can go. I'm not keepin' y'here, it's not kidnap. Y'can go home. It might be better for me, bein' on me own. But d'y'think y'll be safe out on y'own? I mean, I did promise y'old girl that I'd look after the both of yer.'

'Very funny,' Mad Dog said. 'Y'should be on the stage, y'so good. The friggin' landin' stage.'

'Just give it half an hour,' I said.

They both looked down at the floor.

'Listen, there's just one thing we haven't tried,' I said.

'What's that?' Mad Dog said. 'Suicide?'

'No, we haven't asked for a lift yet.'

'An' we're not goin' to, neither.'

'Why not?'

'It's beggin',' Mad Dog said.

'Wha'd'y'think y'do when y'put y'thumb out?'

'It's different,' Half A Dog said.

'No it isn't,' I said.

'Yes it is,' Mad Dog said.

We was all getting at each other.

'Y'all amateurs anyway,' I said. 'Where would y'be without me?'

'Where would we be without you, Bollocks?' Half A Dog said. 'D'y'really want t'know? I'll tell yer where we'd be. We'd all be home in bed. That's where we'd be. Or else we'd be watchin' the telly.'

'It's John Wayne,' Mad Dog said, 'in a cowie.'

'An' then tomorrer we could all watch the game on *Match of the Day*, with our feet up,' Half A Dog said.

'How d'y'know it's goin' t'be on?' I said.

'It's got t'be. It's the only good game.'

'Leeds are playin' Derby, an' Arsenal are at Spurs. That's where the cameras'll be tomorrer. They never go t'Southampton anyway. When was the last time y'saw Southampton at home on the telly? Go on, tell me. They can't put the cameras anywhere, it's such a small ground. The last time they was there, years ago, they had t'stop on the top of the Main Stand, with an umbrella over the cameras and that Kenneth Wolthenstone feller strapped t' the riggin'. If it's windy, y'have t'be pissed t'watch it on the telly.'

'Y'makin' it up.'

'No I'm not,' I said. 'Wait till y'see the ground tomorrer. Only holds about thirty thousand, y've got t'be on a diet t'get in there. Y'll see.'

'On the telly.'

'Go on then,' I said. 'Frig off home now. Go on. There's the stairs, here's y'spud money. Y'should be home for mornin'. I'll run on the pitch at the final whistle an' give the cameras a wave. Except the cameras won't be there.'

'An' we'll wave back at yer,' Half A Dog said, 'except you won't be there neither. Y'll be at home with us, eatin' tea an' toast, or else stuck somewhere down South, in the rain, on y'own.'

'Look,' I said, 'y'can go if y'want. I'm fed up too. But just give it half an hour. Just give it a try, askin' for a lift. It's dead easy after y've done it once. We've got this far, it'd be daft t' turn back now.'

'You go first then.'

'We'll toss for it.'

'Frig off.'

'No, we will.'

'I'm goin' home now, then,' Mad Dog said.

'Mooey,' I said for the second time that night, 'come here.'

He was sitting on the chocolate machine staring out of the window at the lights of the cars going past. I had to shout at him twice.

'We're goin' t'toss up, Moo.'

'What for?'

'Never you mind. Just you call out, "heads" or "tails".'

'Heads or tails.'

'No, Moo, stop kiddin' around now. Just one of them.'

'Heads.'

I flicked the coin up and caught it. I held it up to the light.

'Heads it is, Moo. Well done, you win. You ask first.'

'Eh?'

'The next bloke out of the Transport, you go an' ask him for a lift.'

'What for?'

'So we can get to Southampton.'

'Oh.'

'D'y'understand?'

'I think so. What do I do?'

'Y'walk up to the bloke as he's goin' off to his lorry or his car, an' just as he's about t'get in, y'say t'him, "Is there any chance of a lift, mister?" Have y'got that? "Is there any chance of a lift?"'

'I think so. What do I do then?'

'Well, then he'll either say "yes" or "no". It it's "no" y'tell him he's a boss-eyed bastard an' y'run off. It it's "yes", y'give us the nod an' we'll come up with yer, an' we'll be away.'

'Where'll y'be?'

'Behind a car or a lorry.'

'Why?'

' 'Cos they don't like it if four of us surround them. They get frightened. It's better if it's only one of us at first. An' that's you.'

'Me?' he said.

'That's right. You won the toss.'

'It's funny,' he said, 'I never lose.'

'That's 'cos y've got a lucky face, that's why.'

It wasn't long before the first feller came out of the café. He stood there for a bit where we'd been standing, putting on his gloves. We was in the shadows behind a Pickfords Removal Van, watching him. He lit a ciggie and began walking slowly down the car park. When he got past us, we gave Mooey a shove and he started to follow him. He was tip-toeing in his pumps, with his hands out in front of him, like the Ghost of Christmas Past.

He didn't have far to go. We were watching through the cab windows. The feller stopped, four cars down from us, at a Rover 2000. They're a smart car them. Class. He was fiddling around with his keys when Mooey tapped him on the shoulder. The feller nearly jumped through the window. He turned around quick.

'Wha'd'y'do that for?' he said. He had hold of Mooey by his red and white scarf and his pullover, the one with the egg stains and the holes.

'I dunno,' Mooey said.

'Wha'd't'want, then?'

Mooey was scared out of his mind. You could hear his teeth chattering from where we were.

'Is there any lift of a chance, Mister?'

The feller let Mooey go and give him a good look in the light coming from the floodlights in the car park.

'Yes, y'can come,' he said.

'Wha'?'

'I'm offerin' yer a lift.'

'Oh.'

'Where y'goin' then?'

'Southport,' Mooey said.

The feller laughed. 'Who let you out?' he said.

'They don't know I've gone,' Mooey said.

The feller got the door open and then let Mooey in the passenger door. We stood there waiting for the nod off Mooey. The feller had the engine going before we realized. Mooey was going without us. We ran around from the side of the van. The car was just moving off. We stood in the headlights.

'Hey, what about us?' I shouted.

The car stopped and the feller wound down the window. I could hear Mooey saying. 'Oh yer, I forgot about them. They said t'tell yer, y'were a boss-eyed bastard.'

'Take no notice, Mister,' I said.

He turned back to us. He wasn't very old, a bit older than our Tony. About twenty-five. He had one of them droopy moustaches.

'Is there just you?' he said.

'Yes.'

'Not twenty more behind the van?'

'No, honest.'

'Get in then, an' hurry up.'

'Thanks, Mister,' I said as I grabbed Mooey out of the front seat and pushed him in the back with the others. 'Y're a good skin.'

'It's a nice car, isn't it, Mister?' I said after we'd watched the speedometer for the first ten minutes. None of us had ever gone at a hundred miles an hour before. It was funny, but it didn't seem any faster than doing thirty-five in the laundry van.

'It's not bad is it?' he said.

'Have y'had it long?'

He had a look at his watch.

'About twelve minutes,' he said.

'Hey, go on,' I said. 'Y'haven't just robbed it, have yer?'

The others in the back were all leaning forward, breathing down our necks.

'Now, if I told yer that, an' we got caught, you'd all be accessories after the fact. Y'know what that means, don't yer? Y'd all get into trouble.'

'It's alright,' Mad Dog said. 'We're all on probation anyway.'

'That's what I mean,' the feller said. 'You'd get put away. Sent down.'

'I don't want to get put down,' Mooey said.

'So, I'm not goin' t'tell yer.'

'How did y'manage t'get this far then?' I asked him.

'In a car.'

'What happened?'

'It broke down.'

'Won't they find it on the Motorway an' check the number an' trace it back to you?' I said to him.

'Good question, kidder, you didn't leave y'brains on the pavement, did yer, but the answer, I'm afraid, is no.'

'Why not?'

'That one wasn't mine neither.'

'Bloody hell,' I said, 'here's Clyde, where's Bonny?'

'Y'from the 'Pool, aren't yer?' Mad Dog said after we'd driven along a bit more.

'That's right,' the bloke said, and he winked at me. 'How could y'tell?'

'It was easy. Y'accent give yer away.'

'Hey, y'a smart lad as well, d'y'know that?'

'Arr, it's nothin',' Mad Dog said and sat back in the seat with his arms folded.

94

The feller turned the radio onto Luxembourg after a bit, and I was so buggered that it wasn't long before I fell asleep as we drove along.

MAUREEN LIPMAN

Abscess Makes the Heart . . .

From an early age, well, roughly from the moment the placenta hit the pedal-bin and my mother found there was no way she could return me for a credit note, I realized I needed help with my looks. It was 1946, and the Korean War was news. I had a sallow skin, dark little currant eyes, straight black hair and the refugee jokes flew thick and fast.

My brother, who was described at birth as a 'nose on a pillow' had developed into an infant prodigy with golden curls, courtesy of the 'Twinky' lotion and his mother's rotating finger, and a nose which was normal but pink—with being pushed up into a retroussé by the same finger.

Old Chu Chin Chow's hair resisted everything but gravity and my skin grew used to the ritual torture involved in entering anyone else's home. 'Pinch your cheeks, Maureen,' came the hissed command.

'Why?'

'You look blech' (Yiddish for pasty).

I was eighteen before I dared enter a room without thumbprints on my face.

The second teeth, of course, came out horizontal, and by the age of twelve I'd broken my nose falling down a disused, ornamental well, and my front tooth falling off my bike. I confess to being a dentist's dilemma. They dread seeing me, and the feeling is entirely mutual. The minute I enter the room with the horizontal chair and the red water, I take on a marked resemblance to an Edvard Munch painting, and have been known to scream in an insane fashion when asked to fill in a form. This dates back, like most things in life, to early childhood. For some unaccountable reason, I have always disliked having a big hairy hand in my mouth, hurting me like hell. I know it's foolish, but there you are. It's not for want of trying. I've endeavoured to come to terms with this prejudiced view

96

of dentistry since I gave up having Bonjela rubbed on my gums.

Teeth are a pain in the neck from cradle to coffin (that could have come straight out of *The Penguin Dictionary of Quotations*. And probably did.). Dentistry is a very high-risk occupation. To me especially. I left my last dentist because he believed that Mahler played very loud was an excellent anaesthetic. It obviously was. For him. Towards the end I began fainting as a means of drowning out all three of us.

I blame Him upstairs. How can thirty or so distorted pieces of enamelled ivory thrust their way through the nerve-ends of your skin in a pleasant way? Think how they would feel coming through your feet. Mind you, they'd get about the same wear and tear, but marginally less sugar, I suppose.

I don't remember much about my first teeth, but I vividly recall the permanent (ha!) ones. One day I just looked down and saw two flat, white surfaces looking back. Close scrutiny showed them to be my front incisors which had chosen to grow at an angle of forty-five degrees from their more retiring relatives. To these offending tusks I now realize I owe a debt of gratitude. They taught me to be funny. Ever noticed how many comics have an overbite problem? Make 'em laugh before they punch your teeth in.

For the next ten years it was a question of bracing myself against the world. My mouth looked like the inside of a Sinclair Spectrum. The teeth retreated, paused, fortified themselves and lunged out again, like the Charge of the White Brigade. I even sported a brace when my first boyfriend came home from university. He was awfully understanding, but I only hung on to him by the skin of my teeth.

Nowadays dentists believe in gentle pressure, particularly on the parents' bank account. One of my children models a night-time appliance which goes round the head, looks like a cross between a chasity belt and a BMX biker and appears to work by means of two rubber bands. In the era of the silicon chip, that's progress?

At the age of twelve, demonstrating the non-existent six speeds on my bicycle (Arbonate by name—Bike-Arbonate, geddit?), I jammed on the brakes, transcended the handlebars, and landed on one tooth. I counted to ten and then got up, but the tooth stayed down. And out. Since then my mouth has remained a mystery to me, and every dentist I visit gives the same sharp intake of breath which usually characterizes a visit to a new hairdresser. 'Who *did* this?'

My first dentist had halitosis. Now, as my mother was always saying, 'Breathe on me' before we left the house, in case there was a use for the Milk of Magnesia she kept in her clutch bag, I naturally assumed it was *my* breath that smelled, and consequently tried to hold it for as long as his face was near mine. This led to regular bouts of hyperventilation which were explained away by my being 'highly-strung'.

Another one gave me gas for an extraction. The next thing I remember was the ghastly hissing sound followed by a blood-curdling shriek as the dentist leapt about the surgery, clutching his bleeding hand and screaming 'She bit me, the little shit bit me!'

There's a certain time of day inexorably associated with dentistry. It's about 3.15 in the afternoon. It stems from the middle of Double Geography, when you remembered you were leaving early for 'just a check up' i.e. four hundred fillings and a twenty-minute wince. The feeling was as if a piece of dry cardboard had been inserted in your diaphragm, and it stayed there until you reached the smell of surgery, where it began to thud. Once in the waiting-room, you placed a nine-year-old copy of *Dandy* over your whole face and tried very hard to transmogrify yourself into a rubber plant.

Coronation Day came twice on the days I had my front teeth crowned. My front teeth have been crowned more often than the Habsburgs. The first time was after seeing myself in the film *Up The Junction*. I decided I looked a dead ringer for Arkle, and fled the cinema in search of a tooth-carpenter. The bit I like best in what follows such a decision is the 'shade card'. (This is where your particular shade of tooth is matched up against a chart to avoid the Mix 'n Match look.) The expert flicks past all the whites and creams and settles on mayonnaise yellow as your best blend. Smile, please, you're on yellowvision.

nobody loses all the time

i had an uncle named
Sol who was a born failure and
nearly everybody said he should have gone
into vaudeville perhaps because my Uncle Sol could
sing McCann He Was A Diver on Xmas Eve like Hell Itself
  which
may or may not account for the fact that my Uncle

Sol indulged in that possibly most inexcusable
of all to use a highfalootin phrase
luxuries that is or to
wit farming and be
it needlessly
added

my Uncle Sol's farm
failed because the chickens
ate the vegetables so
my Uncle Sol had a
chicken farm till the
skunks ate the chickens when

my Uncle Sol
had a skunk farm but
the skunks caught cold and
died and so
my Uncle Sol imitated the
skunks in a subtle manner

or by drowning himself in the watertank
but somebody who'd given my Uncle Sol a Victor
Victrola and records while he lived presented to
him upon the auspicious occasion of his decease a
scrumptious not to mention splendiferous funeral with
tall boys in black gloves and flowers and everything and

99

i remember we all cried like the Missouri
when my Uncle Sol's coffin lurched because
somebody pressed a button
(and down went
my Uncle
Sol

and started a worm farm)

e e cummings

The Grange

Oh there hasn't been much change
At the Grange,

Of course the blackberries growing closer
Make getting in a bit of a poser,
But there hasn't been much change
At the Grange.

Old Sir Prior died,
They say on the point of leaving for the seaside,
They never found the body, which seemed odd to some
(Not me, seeing as what I seen the butler done.)

Oh there hasn't been much change
At the Grange.

The governess 'as got it now,
Miss Ursy 'aving moved down to the Green Cow –
Proper done out of 'er rights, she was, a b shame.
And what's that the governess pushes round at nights in the
     old pram?

Oh there hasn't been much change
At the Grange.

The shops leave supplies at the gate now, meat, groceries,
Mostly old tinned stuff you know from McInnes's,
They wouldn't go up to the door,
Not after what happened to Fred's pa.

Oh there hasn't been much change
At the Grange.

Parssing there early this morning, cor lummy,
I' ears a whistling sound coming from the old chimney,
Whistling it was fit to bust and not a note wrong,
The old pot, whistling The Death of Nelson.

No there hasn't been much change
At the Grange,

But few goes that way somehow,
Not now.

Stevie Smith

Poor but Honest

She was poor, but she was honest,
  Victim of the squire's whim:
First he loved her, then he left her,
  And she lost her honest name

Then she ran away to London,
  For to hide her grief and shame,
There she met another squire,
  And she lost her name again.

See her riding in her carriage,
  In the Park and all so gay:
All the nibs and nobby persons
  Come to pass the time of day.

See the little old-world village
  Where her aged parents live,
Drinking the champagne she sends them;
  But they never can forgive.

In the rich man's arms she flutters,
  Like a bird with broken wing:
First he loved her, then he left her,
  And she hasn't got a ring.

See him in the splendid mansion,
  Entertaining with the best,
While the girl that he has ruined,
  Entertains a sordid guest.

See him in the House of Commons,
  Making laws to put down crime,
While the victim of his passions
  Trails her way through mud and slime.

Standing on the bridge at midnight,
   She says: 'Farewell, blighted Love.'
There's a scream, a splash—Good Heavens!
   What is she a-doing of?

Then they drag her from the river,
   Water from her clothes they wrang,
For they thought that she was drownded;
   But the corpse got up and sang:

'It's the same the whole world over;
   It's the poor that gets the blame,
It's the rich that get the pleasure.
   Isn't it a blooming shame?'

Anon.

Exploding Heads

Did I tell you about the day the Head exploded?
      He was up on the stage
      In his usual way
      Hands clasped together
      About to say, *Let us pray* . . .
      When all of a sudden
      Don't know what was the matter
      He went quite berserk
      And grew fatter and fatter . . .

Everyone looked up, their attention riveted on the
expanding figure in front of them.
      He *was* in a state—
      In a terrible tizz,
      His eyes were rotating
      And his tongue it went fizz,
      His knees started knocking:
      Made a terrible row
      And then he blew up
      With a furious Ka-POW!

Well, you can imagine the mess it made.
      .There were bits of his liver
      In the rissoles that day
      And we found both his knees
      When we went out to play.
      Sparrows flew off
      With toes in their beaks
      And bits I won't mention
      Were collected for weeks.

The Deputy looked a bit taken aback by this
unforeseen alteration to the day's timetable . . .
    She tried to think quickly
    Of a suitable hymn
    As she looked at the place
    Where the Head has just been
    'Now, school, we'll sing number
    One hundred and seven:
     For All of Thy Blessings
     We Thank Thee, O Heaven.'

Trevor Millum

House-hunting

The writer and her Dutch composer husband are living in a small rented house in South Wales. They want to buy a house in the West Country which will have enough room for a baby and a grand piano.

Back in South Wales, the house-hunting resumed in earnest. We waited to hear from the West Country estate agents I had rung. Soon our hallway was piled high with information. Photos of jewel-like Cotswold cottages winked out at us from beneath bowers of roses.

'Look at this! Isn't it enchanting! Oh dear, it's seventy-five thousand.'

'And has only two bedroems. It would not be nearlij big enough for my piano—'

'Yes, yes! All right! But if it had only been three times as big and half the price, it would have been perfect!' I gazed longingly at the photographs of Cotswold roses. Early spring had come to our Welsh backyard, and the rusty scrap iron and builders' debris were noticeably not even in bud. . . .

Eventually a real possibility emerged from the welter of Fabergé cottages. The place in question was (now control yourself!) *Apple Tree Cottage*. It had, apparently, a very large attic, big enough for pianos. We approached it with fingers, toes and eyes crossed. It had been uninhabited for a few months, for it was owned by a Mr Fox, whose ancestry was more East End that Cotswold. Mr Fox was that most dangerous form of wild life, the speculative builder. He appeared to be building a bungalow in most of Apple Tree Cottage's garden.

'My word is my bond,' he said, leading us through the low, cottagey ground floor. 'There is a slight smell of damp in here, all right, I admit it straight away, but you can see as well as I can, there's no damp here, it's just that the house hasn't been lived in all winter. A couple of days with the heating on and that smell will disappear, believe you me, trust me, my word is my bond, you can't say fairer than that.'

I was experiencing a strangely schizophrenic sensation. One part of me—lets call it the spoilsport—couldn't help noticing that in the upper rooms the floors bounced slightly as we walked, and crossing the landing, the floorboards beneath my feet crumbled like a particularly delicious school pudding (I was raised in the days when we had school pudding. Nowadays, of course, we hardly even have schools).

The other part of me—let's call it the romantic fool—whispered encouragement. 'Of course the floors are springy! They're so deliciously ooooold! So what if the floorboards crumble? It can be fixed! And look at that lovely view of the dear little garden. If you close your left eye you can't see the new bungalow at all!'

Mr Fox led us to the top floor—a truly enormous barn-like space. You could have got four grand pianos up there, fitted them with motors, and had a Grand Prix. There was the problem of getting the pianos up the narrow cottagey staircase, of course. 'Never mind that!' cried the romantic fool. 'We can take the roof off! All you'll need is a crowbar and a block and tackle! I could do it myself before breakfast!'

'Oh, what a lovely room!' I burst out.

'Perfekt for my workroom,' agreed Van Dyke.

'Yes, you've got two million square feet of space here, easy,' said Mr Fox. 'As you can see, though I say it myself, it's a bargain, really and truly. You can't say fairer than that. I'm robbing myself, you can see that. A young couple came round here this morning and they practically put down a deposit on the spot. I'm telling you this as a friend, Mr Van Dyke—it's only fair you should know. I'm not in this for the money, you see. This transaction is nothing to me. What it is is, I've got too many projects on my hands. So it has to go. The wife loved it. We did think of moving in here ourselves, but, well, you know how it is. I've got too much on my hands.'

I noticed that the mighty beams were pitted with tiny holes. The spoilsport in me reared its ugly head.

'Is there woodworm?'

'I can tell you categorically from me, hand on heart, there is no live woodworm in this entire building,' intoned Mr Fox sepulchrally. 'What you see here is dead holes. If I'd seen live woodworm I'd have treated it, the work of a moment, no sweat. You need have no fears on that score, Mr Van Dyke. My word is my bond. Believe me, you have my word for it.' A patter of light dust fell onto his shoulders.

We skipped to our car and drove off in the grip of a rising hysteria. Van Dyke had, on this occasion, also succumbed to the romantic idiocy. 'It is fantastiek!' he cried. 'There is even roem for—' 'And think how lovely and old it is!' I drooled. 'Mr Fox said four hundred years at least!' Clever Mr Fox. How well he understood us. For a few weeks I dreamed of ancient floorboards, tiny cottage windows, and the garden. Ah, the garden! All right, so it was north facing, about the size of an average bathroom, and shaded by a giant ash tree. Surely there was still room for a rose garden, a vegetable garden, an orchard, and an avenue of pleached hornbeams culminating in a statue of Diana the Huntress?

Soon the Building Society, to whom we had applied for a loan, sent their surveyor off to cast a cold eye on all this glory. And just as Mr Fox had understood us, the Building Society understood Mr Fox. They pointed out that Apple Tree Cottage was only slightly less damp than the North Sea; they drew our attention to the sinister dancing floor, the rotting boards, the worm-infested beams, and the fact that the porch had become detached from the house and was heading off up the hill by itself—a fact which had escaped our notice. They mentioned the bungalow in the garden, and the lack of a kitchen. (Crumbs! That's right! There *wasn't*!) They were prepared to lend us some money towards the purchase. But only enough to buy, as it were, a particularly delicious ice cream.

'The beasts!' I wept. 'We've lost it!'

Mr Fox was most upset. 'This is what you get with these Building Societies, you see, frankly what they're saying is utter rubbish, they're only interested in modern properties, this is simply really and truly not their sort of property. All right, I admit, there's one or two things that want putting right, and I've never said any different, you know me, and I'm quite prepared to do this for you, Mr Van Dyke, this has always been on the cards, and as to the financial side, I'm sure I can fix you up on that score to your satisfaction, my good name has always held me in good stead.'

We decided to start looking again, in Somerset. The cottages down there weren't quite so outrageously sexy, and we might, therefore, get more for our—or rather, *their*—money. So off we went to the pink earth, the airy skies, and the Brendon Hills. We might not even have to buy a house this time, because I knew a dear old lady there who had said I could rent the cottage next door to hers. So I took Van Dyke down there, praying for him to be as ravished as I had been by the little white cottage by the rushing stream, the hanging woods and the red earth, which turned everything pink: even the sheep.

'Oh, look! There's the Quantocks!' I cried in rapture.

'Who? Friends of yours?' he inquired, braking suddenly and smiling obligingly at the nearest yokels. Yes, we were still having the occasional failure of communication. Like all Dutchmen, he spoke English much better than I did, but the thorny question of idiom was a real difficulty. When my mother asked him if he was peckish, he wasn't at all sure whether he was or not. Sometimes it was touch and go. ('Touch aand goe?')

'Look at the red earth! Isn't the garden lovely! Oh, my God, how marvellous: there's a bird!'

Van Dyke looked instead at the inside of the cottage, with a careful Dutch measuring sort of look which made my blood run cold. 'Excuse me, but whejre is my graand piano goijng to goe?' I saw his point. The cottage was two up, two down, and even a quite pixie-ish couple would have to take it in turns to yawn and stretch. It was clear that any grand piano would have to have at least one leg permanently in the garden. In fact, we'd probably have more room if we lived in the grand piano itself.

'Aand if we haav a babje, we will need even moer roem.'

'Oh, I don't know. Babies aren't very big, are they? It could go under the grand piano.' I could see I was beat, though.

Van Dyke very cleverly took me off to a dear little harbour town called Watchet, from which, I discovered, the Ancient Mariner had set sail. Here we had fish and chips. Van Dyke soon discovered that a mixture of chips and literary associations could rouse me from the deepest depression.

'Never mind,' I chirped, already up to the hairline in salt and vinegar, 'it was much too small, you're right.'

'I get klaustrophobia onder such low ceilings.'

'Yes. So do I. Besides, I bet it's miles from the nearest Safeway's.'

So . . . where were we going to live? I was already getting quite attached to the chip shop, but even I could see that there wasn't nearly enough room for the grand piano—unless it was filleted, that is. Not a bad idea, in fact. You'd get eight octaves of fish fingers, for a start. 'C Bass and chips, please, and make it allegretto!'

Since we were in Watchet we dropped in to the local estate agent's, just to have a look. It's a habit that's hard to shake off even after you've found your house and completed your move. Like married men eyeing up other women, I still cast half-interested looks into estate agents' windows. And on this occasion what did we see but the House of our Wildest Dreams. Yes, again.

It was a huge rambling place, with a seventeenth-century back part which had once been (get this) a *sea captain's cottage*, and a most elegant early eighteenth-century front with the original Queen Anne windows, shutters, fireplaces, alcoves, mouldings, dados, ha-has and doo-dahs. Admittedly, the present inhabitants had made a few changes. The attic rooms were full of old mattresses: the outbuilding (our potential Granny annexe) piled high with bits of old railway carriages and plates of raw meat.

If you're breeding deerhounds, of course, you do need a fair amount of meat. You also need a place for them to run about, and that, no doubt, was why they had concreted over the entire back garden and strung up lots of chainlink fencing. But what of that? The romantic fool was back in the driving seat. 'Never mind that concrete,' she whispered. 'A morning with a hammer and chisel and that'll all be gone. And look at those lovely high walls! Yes, a walled garden! Wouldn't Madame Gregoire look glorious sprawling up there? Listen to the seagulls! And just think: you're only twenty seconds' walk from the fish-and-chip shop.'

We did notice that the roof appeared to be covered with a tarpaulin and kind of *glued down*, but the vendor, a charming lady who spent most of her time running after the deerhounds with a shovel assured us that the tarpaulined roof was quite common in the area. 'We couldn't afford to have it done properly,' she said. But I'm sure that was just a figure of speech.

We took a last, feverish look at the house and drove away, speechless with longing. I drew several detailed plans transforming the garden from a waste of concrete and chainlink fencing to something little short of Versailles. In my mind's eye I saw the theoretical baby toddling by the sea. It was all so painfully exciting that we couldn't sleep properly for weeks.

The Building Society's surveyor found it exciting, too. So exciting that he took one look at the tarpaulined roof and ran back to his car, cringing all the way. The Building Society said sorry, they couldn't lend us the price of a single roof tile this time, but they had deferred their usual survey fee and were only charging us £14. (I wish I were a surveyor, don't you? Running back to your car at £28 a minute seems like pretty good money to me.)

We were heartbroken. Like disappointed lovers, we vowed never to look at another house again, but to live, instead, like Diogenes, in a barrel. When we visited my parents in Gloucestershire, and they suggested we look at a couple of houses in the nearby town, we couldn't summon the emotional energy. But we went off, all the same, to be polite. This time, though, we were looking at Victorian semis, not rural ruins. The first house left us cold. The second was all wrong. But the third . . .

Ah, the third. Though I had vowed never again to fall in love with a house, one glimpse of its manly, jutting gables was enough. While it was clearly mortgageable, it was also full of Gothic grandeur.

Well, when I say *grandeur*, it is only a four-bedroomed semi. The sort of place Dracula might well have retired to when the Biting had to Stop. Surrounded by deep gloomy evergreens, crowned by beetling gables (and when I say *beetling* . . . but more of that anon), it boasted long rusting Transylvanian window latches, and not just mullions but *crumbling* mullions.

The great thing about limestone is that it falls to bits so quickly. You don't need gales. Just a few sparrows fluttering up and down around the facade for a year or two, and, my dear, the limestone simply *drops off* in great flakes leaving the whole house with that pitted-by-Civil-War-cannonballs look, even if it was only built in 1906.

Enraptured by the exterior, we crossed the threshold and negotiated the dank flagstones of the hall. Dank flagstones! Imagine! One expected at any moment to see the satanic shade of young Laurence Olivier glide past, wild-eyed, muttering *Rebecca*! or *Cathy*! in an anguished undertone. Within the house was the Heart of Darkness. The Arts and Crafts builders of 1906, who had adorned it with built-in dressers and Art Nouveau fireplaces, had apparently forgotten about windows. The present occupant had reacted to the pervasive gloom by painting the rooms toad brown, slime green, varicose blue and black. On the principle, I suppose, that if you can't beat it you may as well join it.

We fumbled our way around in the dark ('This wall feels quite nice, darling . . . darling?'). We bruised ourselves on delightful architectural details. And best of all, we failed to perceive any serious structural defects. In fact, we failed to perceive anything at all except the wonderful Gothic atmosphere.

By the time we blinked our way into the sunshine outside the back door, we were fatally enchanted. *Do Go Up the Garden*, encouraged the vendor, and so we set off, though it soon became clear we were fatally ill-equipped without crampons and oxygen cylinders. But we did not notice the Himalayan gradient, nor the lack of shed, greenhouse, garage, or even, dammit, path. This was because the lavender was out and great murmurations of bees hung about us. *O the lavender*! *O the bees*! was the order of the day.

From the top of the garden we gazed down, panting, upon the house, and anyone with any sense would have taken this opportunity of noticing the missing tiles, the cracked roof-verges, and the tottering chimneys. We of course, gazed beyond these trivial details to the blue hills. *O the hills*! I cried. This was IT. I felt it in my bones. Third time lucky. We duly applied to the Building Society. This time, surely, they would come up with the goods. After all, it was a surburban semi. What more did they want?

The Building Society was, of course, outrageously rude about Romantic No.21. They demanded that we root out the rot, scoop up the slime and, worst of all, shoot the woodworm. 'Isn't there room for us and the woodworm in God's creation?' I wailed. But apart from demanding a long list of repairs, they did appear to be willing, thank God, to push the necessary cash our way. No.21 was all but ours. Immediately I began to feel deeply attached to South Wales. The dear builders' yard at the back! Who would take care of it? Would it feel lonely?

No.21 wasn't really what we had expected to end up with: a suburban semi in a small town. But as suburban semis go, it *was* the nearest thing to Elsinore. What's more, though the town (Stroud) was a town, it wasn't much of a town. Up at our end the pavements get a bit half-hearted and the trees get more arrogant. Besides, it did strike us as convenient that it was only a few minutes' walk from the bank, the post office, and — to be fearlessly frank and honest — the Maternity Hospital.

J.P.DONLEAVY

At Longitude and Latitude

They thought I was crazy when I bought the island. I said it was a bargain. And got one of these unsinkable rubber rafts. They asked me was I worried about sharks. What a laugh. I said what are you blind? Can't you see I've got this new type harpoon? Any of these sharks come near me, he gets it right between the eyes.

Then they said I'd starve. So I told them about the deep freeze with mutton, chops and beef. I could even freeze soup. And just in case, I had my handbook for survival that tells you about chewing bark.

So on an afternoon in June I set sail. They were all there on the dock watching me. Wise guys making cracks about wait till the hurricane. I know the type, just trying to get the wind up me. So I waved the weather report right in their faces. I said read this, it says clear sailing and besides maybe you're just jealous because I'm going to be nice and lonely for a couple of months listening to my portable gramophone. I think, deep inside me, I hated them all anyway. All the kind of guys who lob balls into the sun when you're playing tennis.

The sky was bright and clear blue, the outboard motor purring away. It was twenty-two miles. In maybe three hours with a good current, I'll be able to see the little hill with the palm trees and where I fixed the flag pole. That was another thing they were beefing about, they thought it was anarchy to fly my own personal flag and that the coast guard would think it was distress or something. When it was only me.

About three thirty there was a slight westerly breeze and a few clouds. I thought just a touch of right rudder. A few of them said they would come out late this afternoon in Harold's cruiser just to see if maybe I sprung a leak and had to use the rubber raft. They won't leave me alone. But there's no sign of anybody. And there's no other island like mine anywhere in these parts. Somehow they just don't want to see a guy go off to be by himself. Always have to make out he's a jerk or his politics want to be watched.

I figure I ought to be coming in sight any minute now, although it's taking longer than I expected. And when you're out here all alone you get ideas. Maybe a little left rudder. I can't wait to get up a good charcoal fire and singe up a nice thick steak. I always say, a few hours at sea brings on an appetite.

When I bought it I thought the guy was asking too much but he said he'd throw in the boat as well as the diesel generator and enough oil to last a year. He told me he wasn't the introspective type although you sure could do some serious thinking on that island and the fishing was great. So I thought with electricity, water converter and shower, what more could I want except to get away from Harold and the others for a few months. And Harold's wife made that nasty remark that I didn't know any of them anymore since I took the speech improvement course. There's nothing wrong with making sure you're never misunderstood and I think being able to communicate ideas clearly ought to be uppermost in anybody's mind.

The way I figure I ought to be there by now. Maybe it's just this slight overcast. I feel like a shower and shave and then a nice can of beer in the hammock and tune into shore for some dance music. And I'll put out the string of coloured lights tonight. Wonderful how they give you that festive feeling.

I think more left rudder. Might have miscalculated this current. This sea is some size. I'm just a needle in a haystack out here. At the beach picnic Myrtle showed she just couldn't take it, getting sore when I slipped the fish down her back. Must be sorry now she called me a boor. She'd probably like to come stay on the island but I'm inviting none of them.

Maybe I better try right rudder. Not a sign of shore anywhere. And its getting dark. This calls for checking position. My God. I'm here. It's gone.

JILL TWEEDIE

Dear Mary

Dear Mary

Last week (reason why I didn't write) I got these agonizing pains, at least seven of them. My gums swelled up all along the molars, the glands under my chin felt like loose ball-bearings, my stomach took off for foreign parts, with only the occasional letter home, and the parts of me left behind got fed into a concrete mixer. Josh, I said. Do you ever get a pain so painful that if it went on longer than a quarter of a second, your nails would fall out? The flickery sort of pain, Josh, the kind that flashes up the soles of your feet, tunnels through your ribcage, streaks across your neck and explodes out of your left ear? The kind that makes you think God is skewering you for a celestial shish kebab? No, said Josh. But *Josh*, I said. Don't you ever get a very *small* pain? Even the teeniest twinge in, say, the third metatarsal from the right or just under your nosebone? No, he said. Sometimes I think I am married to someone not of flesh and blood at all. Sometimes I think they ran up Josh in some laboratory, wodged him together out of a strange, thick substance, like pressed-felt carpet tiles.

I couldn't even call the doctor, due to the fact that Kev is back and stripping the wallpaper from the bedroom wall. You remember Kev, who kept seeing the Royal Family on our ceiling? Marf, he said when he arrived at the door. They give me ESP in that place and I'm cured. Now he only sees Princess Anne's baby and that only occasionally, in the odd bit of wallpaper. Which, considering he saw the Queen, the Duke, Princesses M and A and Princes C, A and E before, is pretty well a cure by any standards. So Kev's large as life again, showering plaster down on the two of us, making me look like a long-dead corpse. If the doctor did come, he'd only diagnose lead poisoning or some other variation on what might be called a Decorational Disease.

117

Poor Jane had to cope with the baby because she's still on holiday till next week. I say 'poor Jane' but, actually, she'd got herself perfectly organized. She'd dump a bowl of shredded wheat on my tummy at 9 a.m. and then take off, baby and Rover and all, to her friends in this squat. The baby arrived back every evening looking like he'd been forked out of an allotment, like a new potato. He was just one staggering smut. Jane, he's *filthy*, I'd say in shock horror. Yeah, she'd say he is, isn't he? She didn't seem to care at all, she seemed to think that it didn't matter, babies being filthy, because of them being washable and pre-shrunk and permanently-pleated. I got this nasty redundant feeling, especially since the only thing I could see through the grime were the baby's teeth, exposed in a blissful grin.

Why did Doctor Spock never reveal that all babies want in life is squats and filth? I reckon it's a capitalist conspiracy to keep mothers in the home buying 20 different varieties of baby-cleaning products. The advertisers hire troops of evil little gnomes to impersonate kiddies who like being washed and eating wholewheat muesli and Marmite, when all the time what really makes them happy is grovelling about in dirt munching old potato peelings.

It's a conspiracy that has put a stone on me. I dare say if I wasn't so fat, I'd feel less pain—obviously, the more there is of you, the more lebensraum germs have to work in. My trouble is, I don't think I'm a teapot, I think I'm a dustbin. I have this overwhelming urge to fill myself with left-overs. Down the little red lane, I say to the baby and the baby says ugh and down *my* little red lane go the stewed prunes, the pureed spinach, the chicken-and-carrot dinner, the soggy rusks, the chewed banana. *Pour encouragez les autres*. What's more, if anyone ever said to me, Martha, how do you fancy a fry-up of a dried-out pork chop, three cold roast spuds, six limp celery tops and a wedge of mouldy cheese? I'd say not a lot, thanks awfully. But that's what I eat, myself, every time I defrost the fridge. Oh look, world, I say. See what a good, thrifty housewife I am. There's not one left-over in *my* pantry. It's all neatly packed away on my hips.

Josh pronounced my illness psychosomatic, brought on by

refusing to face the fact that I can't get into anything but my bell-bottomed jeans. It's true that nighties are the only garments that flatter me and I suppose you can't be an entirely well person while walking about in nighties. Perhaps I'll marry Kev. His monarchical interests might divert him from marital flab, unless he started seeing Lady Di in the folds of my spare tyre.

Please Keep Off The Grass

A democratic state, they said,
A democratic land.
They printed little gold-edged notes
And hired a silver band.
You may say what you like, they said,
If you do as you're told,
So please keep off the grass, my friend,
In case the grass is sold.

Peter Tinsley

Fiddler on the Roof

A handy spring guide for those wishing to make good the ravages of the worst winter in roofing memory.

Poking Something Dead out of a 4" Soil Elbow Using the Half-hoe and dangling Paperclip Techniques

During the winter, our feathered friends often stand on chimneys, probably to see if there are crumbs in neighbouring gardens. Sometimes, for reasons not always clear to ornithologists, they drop dead, roll down the roof, get lodged in the gutter, and, with the spring thaw, wash into the downpipe and become stuck in the junction with the external soil-pipe, causing unsavoury backwash to sanitary ware and people indoors going around saying 'What's that niff?'

Before, therefore, levering up external drain man-holes with an old hub-cap and poking tied-together golfclubs along the conduits, it is sensible to determine that the fault does not lie with a rotted starling or similar. Go up to the roof-guttering, using an extending ladder and a 137/4b B UPA claim form, and, with a four-foot length of sharpened hoe-handle, poke down hard towards the elbow. With luck, you will impale the corpse and, withdrawing the hoe hand-over-hand, remove it altogether. If you poke too hard, and the downpipe is either plastic or old cast-iron, you may find that the starling comes out through a hole in the elbow, but do not worry, the gap may be quite easily repaired with Harbutt's Plasticine, or, more professionally, with instant glue and a hole-shaped piece of waterproof thingy cut from an old anorak.

If, however, as can happen with any advanced technology, the hoe-handle falls into the downpipe, it may be possible to retrieve the corpse using a piece of ordinary kitchen string with a paperclip affixed to one end and twisted to form a hook. With a fully deteriorated bird, you should be able to lower the hook inside the rib cage and locate it under the sternum; if the feathers and flesh have not yet rotted off, though, try to get the hook around a foot (or 'claw'). It should then draw up easily.

The fallen hoe-handle, in most cases, is best left where it is. The attendant reduction of volume of the downpipe should not cause problems, except in rain, but if water does flood up and over the guttering, it is a simple matter to bang a hole in the guttering and stand an oil drum under it. When emptying the oil drum, do NOT attempt to tip it over (it will weigh half a ton!), simply siphon the water by sucking through a tube cut from garden hose into some other convenient smaller recept-acle, such as a tin bath, from which the water may then easily be emptied with a saucepan.

Replacing Blown-off Roof Tiles without Dangerous Hammering

Tiles are attached to roofs by a complicated system of battens, lugs and titchy little tacks that cannot be held by normal human beings without getting a thumb flattened, often the cause of the hammer sliding down the roof and into a downpipe whence, due to its consistency, it cannot of course be removed with a half-hoe or paperclip. You have to prise the entire length of pipe from the brickwork using a garden spade, which may sometimes break in two. If this happens, do not throw the pieces away: the shovel bit can come in useful for lifting a man-hole cover if your hub-cap is not up to it, and the handle bit can be used for breaking up larger birds, e.g. pigeons, storks, etc. that have got into other downpipes and can be removed only after dismembering.

There is, however, an alternative to all this heavy labour on tiles. That is to use common or garden adhesive tape! Simply tape one end to a new tile with a generous length left hanging and—having climbed up your ladder to the lower end of the pitched roof—push the tile up the roof using a long mop (or, if the missing tile is high-up, a long mop tied to a broom) until it is over the hole. Then, very carefully, flip up the length of hanging tape with the mop so that it is above the hole, and bang at it until it sticks, leaving the new tile secured over the cavity, rather like a flap.

This will of course take a little practice. If the tape does not stick first time and you find the tile hurtling towards you down the slope, put something over your teeth.

Relocating the TV Aerial for Spring Using Only Curtain-rails and a Brick

High winter winds can play havoc with a roof aerial, which may be either VHF or UHF, depending on how much you know about it.

If you start getting flat heads and little legs, there is no need to bother either with expensive know-alls from the Yellow Pages or dangerous ladders. A TV aerial can be turned quite easily from inside the house by attaching an ordinary brick to a fifteen-foot length of metal curtain-rail with a stout rubber band or surgical tape, both available from the normal stockists. Simply choose the window nearest to the chimney holding the aerial, open it, and feed the curtain-rail out, brick-first.

Stand an assistant in the garden who will direct your aim. He should also be able to see a television screen by looking through the window, and wear a tin hat, or, if that is not to hand, a heavy-duty basin. Since the weight of the brick may cause the curtain-rail to wobble a bit, have a few practice runs before committing yourself to the stroke, then, when ready, simply swing the rail upward in the direction of the aerial. The brick will strike the aerial, knocking it into a different position. Eventually, on an agreed signal from your assistant, you will hit on the correct position for perfect pictures, provided the brick does not come off.

Keep the curtain-rail by you. Later in the year, with a sharp meat axe firmly bound to the (far) end, it will be indispensable for pruning remoter twigs...

... Or for Getting Tennis Balls out of Guttering

All pitched roofs are designed to allow tennis balls to roll down them at a speed carefully calculated to ensure that they lodge in a gutter. Quite why this should be cannot be explained except by pointing out that building is a masonic pursuit, and that people prepared to roll up one trouser-leg and throw blancmange at each other should not perhaps be let out during daylight hours.

In any event, spring is a time for going up the ladder with our invaluable curtain-rail and using it to poke the tennis ball out of the guttering. Since all tennis balls are always seventeen feet away from where you thought they were when you looked out of the attic window, this invariably means that you will find yourself laying the curtain-rail inside the gutter, pushing it towards the tennis ball with the full extent of your arm, and giving it one final expertly desperate shove to ensure that (a) the ball flies out, and (b) the curtain-rail stays there, beyond reach.

The best way to get the curtain-rail out is to go down the ladder again and throw the tennis ball at the gutter in the hope that the retaining shackles are rusted enough to allow the gutter to fall away from the roof, bringing the curtain-rail down with it.

They generally are.

Removing a Damaged Chimney Pot without Spending £££s

This winter has been particularly hard on the standard terracotta chimney pot, for a variety of reasons. In many homes, the cold weather has persuaded people that there is nothing quite like a good old-fashioned fire, which has meant that even some expert handymen have occasionally got into trouble through refusing to be defrauded by ratfaced opportunist scum offering to clean chimneys, and preferring to do it themselves.

The method is quite simple. An ordinary household broom is fixed to half a hoe-handle, which in turn is stoutly roped to a length of flexible curtain-rail connected to an old mashie by any adhesive tape you happen to have left over from tiling. This is then fed up the chimney until the broomhead, being oblong, wedges in the chimney pot. A few sharp bangs should then bring all the soot down. This, however, may, upon close inspection, turn out to have a few terracotta shards in it, and the wise workman would be well advised to complete the job by knocking the chimney off.

Alternatively, damage can also result if, by sheer mischance, the attempt to improve BBC2 reception falls prey to a sudden treacherous gust, and the brick swings back with half a chimney following it. In this case, too, the meticulous expert will wish to remove the remains rather than, say, have birds fly into its sharp edges and roll dying into his downpipes. Where roofs are concerned, one must anticipate every eventuality.

How, though, is one to go about it? We have all listened to those so-called professionals who maintain there is nothing for it but to climb a ladder and set to work with a pick-axe, but those of us who have tried lashing out with a pick-axe tied to a curtain-rail know just how awkward that can be, especially when neighbours discover the exact nature of what is sticking out of their Volvo roof.

Nor, for the same reason, should one simply stand on the garage and shy rocks at the thing. One should stand on the garage and attempt to get a rope around it. Not, it must be stressed, a lasso, which, though undeniably romantic, lies beyond the expertise of even the keenest, but a simple strand of sashcord, thrown over the roof and caught by an assistant standing on the other side, i.e. in the road, who can then throw it back so that a loop is formed around the chimney. It is sensible to attach a brick to the thrown end of the rope to facilitate its flight, and it would thus be a wise precaution to cordon the road off briefly at each end, in case (a) the assistant misses the brick and it strikes a passing motorist or (b) the assistant attempts to catch the brick and is run over by a passing motorist. (*The best way to cordon a road off is to make little tripods, with any bits of hoe- and spade-handles you may have in your workshop, and stretch a length of curtain-rail between them.*)

Once the loop is in position, a sharp tug should bring the damaged chimney tumbling safely down the roof, dislodging no more than a few tiles which can be taped back into position, along with any guttering, downpipes, TV aerials, and so forth.

If a sharp tug is not sufficient to remove it, however, your wisest course would be to relocate the rope ends so that they hang down on the road side of the house, attach them to your rear bumper, and drive off slowly.

You will now discover the wisdom of not using the pickaxe. With luck, your neighbours will be prepared to run you to the station in the Volvo, until your car is back from the body-shop.

F*ollow On*

January 1943 – At Sea

Before Reading

● What do you normally expect from a war story, or from war memoirs? What is the difference between the two?

During Reading

● Apart from the humour, it is the amount of precise detail which is noteworthy. Jot down half a dozen examples.

After Reading

● Write the letter which Milligan might send home, having arrived in Algiers.

● Describe the voyage from the point of view of one of the seasick soldiers or one of the naval officers.

● Continue the memoirs in a similar style.

● One of the most noticeable aspects of the writing is the precision of the detail. Imagine that you were once involved in a war. Look back at a time during your involvement when nothing much was happening in the way of military action. Write your memoirs of that time, giving attention to detail wherever it is appropriate.

● Milligan mixes truth with fiction, as we can see more clearly in this extract from earlier in the book:

It was a proud day for the Milligan family as I was taken from the house. 'I'm too young to go,' I screamed as Military Policemen dragged me from my pram, clutching a dummy. At Victoria Station the RTO gave me a travel warrant, a white feather and a picture of Hitler marked 'This is your enemy.' I searched every compartment, but he wasn't on the train. At 4.30, June 2nd, 1940, on a summer's day all mare's tails and blue sky we arrived at Bexhill-on-Sea, where I got off. It wasn't easy. The train didn't stop there.

Choose an incident from your own life to write about. The main skeleton of the story should be true, but the flesh you put on it can be as fictional as you like.

● Interview a friend or a relative about their memories of the Second World War. It might be useful to have a list of things to ask them (evacuation – air-raids – rationing, etc.) but be prepared to abandon your list and follow up on things of interest which the interviewee mentions. Write this up as an article for a magazine and give a copy to the person you interviewed.

Unreliable Memoirs

Before Reading

● These extracts are taken from a book called *Unreliable Memoirs*. How reliable would you expect memoirs to be?

During Reading

● Is there anything to suggest which part of the world the writer comes from?

After Reading

● Do any of the teachers you know have eccentricities (i.e. something more than the usual peculiarities)? Write a character study of one of your teachers from junior school (it's probably wiser – and safer – than using someone from your present school). Consider their looks, behaviour, particular habits and one or two noteworthy incidents.

● The author is good at describing people:

A novel rearrangement of his lips took place which I guessed to be a smile. The teeth thereby revealed featured eye-catching areas of green amongst the standard amber and ochre.

though some are not very subtle:

A pig born looking like him would have demanded plastic surgery.

Pick out any other striking phrases or sentences which describe people in these two extracts. Which are the most effective?

● Some of the author's comparisons are also very striking:

Wreathed by dense smoke and lit by garish flames, the stunned Mr Ryan looked like a superannuated Greek god in receipt of bad news.

Choose five people you know, as varied a selection as possible, and describe each of them using a comparison. Aim to communicate your pictures of these people to a reader who has never met them.

● Are there some subjects at which you are particularly bad—or in which you can remember doing something daft or incompetent?

Write about yourself in that lesson *from the teacher's point of view.*

● How do people like Ronnie the One behave in civilian life? Do they act in the same way at home, in shops, in cafes? Write a sketch or short play set in a civilian situation in which Ronnie the One is a character. (You might like to include Peebles as well. Imagine Ronnie the One in a restaurant giving his order to the waiter who is Peebles – or vice versa!)

● Discuss these descriptions of the writer and put them in order of accuracy:
— he disapproved of the army—he was a pacifist
— he was popular with the other soldiers
— he was a coward – he was brave
— he wanted to get by with the least trouble
— he wasn't any good at drill or presentation of kit
— he respected Ronnie the One—he wanted to be an officer.

The Loaded Dog

Before Reading

● Just what might the title mean? How many alternatives can you suggest?

During Reading

● Pause at the end of the paragraph which begins, 'Run, Andy! Run!' How do you think the story will continue?

After Reading

● Draw a diagram and write clear instructions for: (a) making a cartridge; (b) making the special cartridge Andy and Dave constructed in order to blow up the fish. Make sure you show the differences between the two.

● Animal characters:
—Work with a partner. The first person should write down one fact about the dog's character and pass the paper to his or her partner, who will add another fact. Keep doing this until you've exhausted the information available. Write up the points you've listed in a paragraph titled 'Tommy'.
—Working on your own, write a paragraph about any animal which *you* know. Start by jotting points down in a list.

● As long as no one is badly hurt, accidents can often make amusing stories. Animals, especially pets, also provide good material for

128

stories. 'The Loaded Dog' is lucky in being able to combine both. *Either* write an account of an accident which happened to you or to someone you know, *or* write about an incident involving a pet. If you can think of a story which involves both, so much the better! Be sure to make the most of any parts which are funny.

● Due to an amazing advance in technology, it has become possible to interview dogs by implanting a CanineChatPak in their brains. This was difficult with Tommy as his brain was rather small but the dedicated scientific team eventually succeeded. *Either* write the interview between the TV chat show host/hostess and Tommy about the cartridge incident *or* act out the interview in pairs. If you could work in threes, one person could record the interview using a notepad or tape-recorder.

● You are Tommy. Write the thoughts that go through your head on that fateful day. Please don't bark during the lesson. Or write your thoughts and feelings as a kind of free-form poem:

My name is Tommy
I live in the bush.
I've got three friends
Called Andy, Dave and Jim –
They think they're clever
But I'm not taken in . . .

● Write a sketch or a cartoon strip which involves Tommy, the yellow dog, and any of the other dogs mentioned. It could be about the events recounted in 'The Loaded Dog' or some other story which you make up. You might like to introduce a 'guest' into your story, such as Gnasher from the *Dennis the Menace* strip.

Goat's Tobacco

Before Reading

● How much of the past is it possible to remember without the assistance of a written record? How much can one person's memory hold? (Is there a limit?)

During Reading

● Roald Dahl writes for both adults and children. Which audience do you think he has in mind when you read this extract?

After Reading

● Discuss which other titles might suit this passage; for example:
Come-uppance
Taking the Doctor Down a Peg
Practical Joke
Nothing Like a Good Pipe
Mischief with Muck
Would it have been better not to give away the main point of the story in the title?

● What happened next? Write the conversation which then took place between the ancient half-sister, the manly lover and the mother.

● Humour often comes from contrast. In this story the contrast is between the rather self-satisfied and pompous man returning from his swim and the coughing and choking figure a few moments later. Pick out some of the phrases from before and after which are most effective in making this contrast. For example:

Before
Chest out, strong and virile, healthy and sunburnt

After
His face was as still and white as virgin snow and his hands were trembling

● Would the manly lover have seen the funny side of it later? What is the best way of dealing with a joke at your expense? Write a scene or (working in pairs) devise a short sketch in which one of the characters manages to cope with a practical joke. You could follow this with 'How not to deal with a practical joke'.

● In the introduction to *Boy* from which this chapter is taken, Roald Dahl writes:

An autobiography is a book a person writes about his own life and is usually full of all sorts of boring details. This is not an autobiography. I would never write a history of myself. On the other hand, throughout my young days at school and just afterwards a number of things happened to me that I have never forgotten. None of these things is important, but each of 'em made such a tremendous impression on me that I have never been able to get them out of my mind. Each of them, even after a lapse of fifty and sometimes sixty years, has remained seared on my memory . . . Some are funny. Some are painful. Some are unpleasant. I suppose that is why I have always remembered them so vividly. All are true.

Talk to someone who is twenty or thirty years older than you and ask them what they remember about their days at school. Are the things they remember funny, painful or unpleasant? You can report back on what you discovered to the rest of your group.

Go back to the person you talked to (with a tape-recorder or pencil and notepad) and find out more about one particular time or incident in their life so that you can write 'One Chapter in the Life of . . .'

● The writer says, 'All are true'. Obviously no one could remember the exact conversation that took place fifty years ago, so how true is true? How much detail can be made up before a story stops being true? (See the "Follow On" section to the extract from Spike Milligan's memoirs—and note the title of Clive James's autobiography).

Where Did our Pete Find this Tiger?

Before Reading

● What reactions do you have after reading the first sentence?

During Reading

● What kind of people do the writer and her family seem to be? Jot down your impressions as you read through.

After Reading

● Of which member of the family (apart from the writer) do you have the clearest impression? What do you know about that person? What can you guess about him or her?

● The family in the story is obviously used to having neighbours taking a close interest in what goes on. How well do you know the people next door to you? The people slightly further away? Imagine one day it is revealed that one of your neighbours was actually a pop star/millionaire/Mafia boss/spy/dictator-in-exile/skunk farmer (or whatever) and a reporter comes to talk to you. Work in pairs and interview each other. Base your answers on someone you actually know, and make up what you don't know. This can be recorded and/or written up afterwards.

● Convert any section of the extract into a radio or TV play. If you write it as a radio play you must remember that everything must be conveyed in what the characters *say*. If you write it as a TV play remember to describe what is being shown as well as what is being said.

● Tell someone else about a time when you had an accident (or, if you've never had one, an illness). They should then write up your verbal description into a written account. Check that they have got the facts straight before they make a final copy of it.

● Write a description of a pet based on close observation of its actual appearance and behaviour. Record its looks, its character and its habits. Don't be afraid to use comparisons. Give your description to someone else and get them to underline the words, phrases or lines they like most. Using those parts, and cutting out anything which is not essential, work them into an unrhymed poem. Here is an example of how one girl made a poem like this:

> My cat is as vain as a film star or a queen
> like Cleopatra. She purrs like she has an
> engine deep down in her throat or her chest
> and her evil green eyes shine in her face
> like emeralds. She miaows pathetically and
> gets ignored or fed. But later behind her
> half-closed eyelids she dribbles in contentment.
> She sleeps all day, lazy as a cow but I suppose
> she's as gentle and as gracious as a ballerina
> when she wants to be. When she walks along
> the wall it's as if she's a tightrope walker on
> padded paws. When she's asleep she's just like any
> other furry fat cat.

Her final version went like this:

> Smug and vain like
> Cleopatra,
> Deep in her throat her
> Engine purrs and
> Evil green eyes shine
> Like emeralds.
> Behind half-closed
> Eyelids,
> Dribbling in contentment
> Lazy as a cow—
> But gentle and gracious
> Like a ballerina:
> She is a tightrope walker
> On padded paws.

● Write an article for a magazine on pets. There are plenty of articles written about how to keep your budgie healthy and ways of grooming your goldfish, but you should aim for something more controversial. Try to get your readers to ask themselves whether it's right to have pets, for instance. Find out (from the RSPCA, for instance) about unwanted and abandoned pets. How much is spent on pet foods each year? Why do people have pets? Is it a modern trend? Is it cruel to keep birds and small animals in cages? (There are plenty of questions to ask—be prepared for some emotional reactions!)

● Write about the incident where the kitten is brought home from the point of view of Prince.

Snake in the Grass

Before Reading

● What does the phrase 'snake in the grass' mean?

During Reading

● Pause after '. . . My Old Man's a Dustman'. What impression have you got of Robin so far?

After Reading

● What happens next?

● Make a list of the characters and note what happens to each of them as a result of what Robin does. For example:
His father—wet trousers, bloodstained shirt, broken glasses . . .

● Write the story of the trip to Miller's Beck from the point of view of one of the other characters. You will need to bring out the way that character feels about Robin.

● Discuss these questions with a partner:
— How old do you think Robin is?
— Is he believable? (Are there children as awful as he is?)
— Does it matter whether he is entirely believable or not?
— Does this type of story depend on a certain amount of exaggeration?
— Is exaggeration common in funny stories?
— How common is it in our everyday speech? ('I've told you a million times . . . don't exaggerate!')
— Why does Robin behave as he does?
— What is your opinion of the behaviour of the adults in the story?
— What advice would you give them?
— Sometimes we are on the side of 'naughty' characters, for example, William in the stories by Richmal Crompton. (Why?) Are we on Robin's side? (If not, why not?)

● Write a story, true or fictional, about a child who is a real pain!

You may decide to write about several instances of the child's behaviour – but concentrate most of your attention on one particular event.

● Why are some children naughtier than others? Is it their personality or the way they have been brought up—or both? Decide what you think about these questions before you tackle the next assignment.

● That evening, Robin's mother and father discuss their son. Write their conversation. Do this in prose or play form.

A Night on the Mountain

Before Reading

● Research some of the history of the North American Indians, especially the Cherokee, and the treatment of such people by the European settlers.

During Reading

● Stop after reading the first five paragraphs. What have you deduced about the writer and his granpa? How do they seem to feel about white men?

● A 'still' is a place where spirits like whisky (whiskey is the American and Irish spelling) are made. Make a note of any other expressions which may be new to you as you read through the story.

After Reading

● Compare your list of expressions with others. Work out the meanings as far as you can and check the remainder with the teacher (who may or may not know, but will be able to suggest likely explanations).

● List the details which the writer states about the appearance of the two strangers. Divide your list into details which show the men in a negative way (e.g. 'his eyes looked slitted, way back in swelled-up fat'), a neutral way ('Mr Slick had a little mustache') and a positive way.

● Little Tree does not realize the full meaning of some of the things the two men say. This is the source of some of the humour in the story. Find some examples of this.

● What words would best describe Little Tree?

resourceful   thrifty   honest
energetic   innocent   vengeful
loyal   cunning   obedient

Pick the three most appropriate or use words of your own. Compare your list with others in your group and see what level of agreement there is.

● Because we experience what occurs through the eyes of the boy, we are not told directly what happens. Why *are* the two men there? What happens to them? Why and how does it happen?

● *'Granpa had learnt me not to interrupt when people was talking'*.
Forrest Carter writes the story as Little Tree would speak it, even though the grammar is unusual. Most adults, apart from writers, get upset when pupils write just as they speak, yet often such writing is far more lively and readable than that which is grammatically correct. This is an issue which you and your teacher should discuss.
Try the following assignments:
— Interview someone using a tape-recorder and then write down exactly what they said. Compare interviews with others in the class and see how 'grammatical' they are.
— Think of an incident in your own life and tell it to a friend. Get them to record it. Now write it down exactly as you told it, including the unfinished sentences and 'ums' and 'ers'.
What conclusion do you draw about the way Forrest Carter writes?

● What does this story have in common with 'Goat's Tobacco'?

Thoughts on Paper

Before Reading

● Are parents always a problem? Can they help it?

During Reading

● How many times does Maria Morris switch topic? Is there usually a link between the topics she covers?

After Reading

● What is Maria Morris's style of writing most like—a letter to a friend, a phone call to a friend, a talk to a friend, or what? Do you think she would be a good friend?

● Imagine you are Maria's mother or father and write an account of your feelings in a similar style to Maria's.

● Jot down the things Maria says which you agree with and, in a separate list, the things you disagree with or are not sure about. Compare your lists with a partner and see how similar your reactions were.

● Does she complain too much? Covering the same kinds of topics that Maria deals with, write a piece in a similar style but taking the opposite point of view to Maria wherever possible.

● Prepare an article for a magazine on the topic of 'Parents' by thinking about the following questions and researching the answers to those which you find difficult. Don't rely on your own experience – ask other people.
— Is it possible to grow up without disagreements with your parents?
— In which relationship does the most conflict occur: mother – daughter, mother – son, father – daughter or father – son?
— Did your parents have similar disagreements with their parents?
— What about your grandparents?
— What tends to happen in other cultures?
— What was the relationship like between children and parents one hundred years ago? Five hundred years ago?
— How do you think you would behave if you had children of your own?

From all your notes, decide the four or five most important or interesting points. Write each one down in a simple sentence. Put the sentences in a sensible order. Now write a paragraph to back up what you have said in each of the sentences.

● You can adopt a similar approach to other subjects. One which Maria Morris tackles briefly is examinations. You can draw up a similar list of questions to the ones about parents and conflict: Is it possible to do without exams; what happened in other periods of history; how did your grandparents cope with exams, and so on.

● Write a sketch about parent – child conflict set in another period of history; for example, Neanderthal Girl comes home late to the cave or Eric the Viking disapproves of his son's hairstyle.

● Write a sketch or a story in which examinations do not have anything to do with jobs or careers but have to be taken for everyday activities such as eating, drinking and walking.

● 'We're always expected to have . . . ' In small groups, write down what you feel is expected of a girl in today's society. Do the same for what is expected of a boy. Compare your lists and draw up a combined list for the group. How many of the items would you be happy to see crossed off? What would it be like if there were no expectations?

Southward Bound

Before Reading

● What image do you have of Liverpool and Liverpudlians? Where have your ideas about Liverpool come from?

During Reading

● When do you think *Scully* was written?

After Reading

● Choose a section of the extract to turn into a script for radio. Remember that everything you wish the listener to know has to be said by one of the characters or made clear by sound effects. Read the scripts in small groups and then record one or two of them.

● The driver of the Rover is stopped by the police while Scully and friends are in the car. *Either* write the statement which Scully makes to the police *or* the conversation which takes place when the boys are questioned.

● Several years later, Scully is driving out of a motorway service area and sees a group of hitch-hikers. He stops to give them a lift. Continue the story from there.

● Do you find Scully a likeable character or not? How close is he to your image of a Liverpudlian? Try listing his good and bad points, starting like this:

Good points   **Bad points**
quick-witted   *bossy*

● *'An' we'll wave back at yer,'* Half A Dog said, *'except you won't be there neither. Y'll be at home with us, eatin' tea an' toast, or else stuck somewhere down South, in the rain, on y'own.'*

Like Forrest Carter, Alan Bleasdale tries to write speech in a way which will be realistic. Work on these questions with a friend:
— How successful is he in making the speech realistic?
— Do you find it difficult to read?
— Is it necessary to write speech like this?
— Which characters in other extracts or stories in this book have def-

137

inite regional accents?

— On what occasions might a person's accent matter?

— Which accents do you find difficult to understand when you hear them?

— Everyone has an accent—how would you describe yours?

● Using whichever form you choose (short story, play, radio script, etc.) give an account of the evening experienced by the people in the Zodiac, starting before Scully and his friends encounter them and continuing afterwards.

● Tell the story of the boy from Ulverston Grammar School.

Abscess Makes the Heart . . .

Before Reading

● What might this extract be about?

During Reading

● You may come across words which you don't recognize. Don't worry about them – jot them down and look them up or get them explained afterwards. (Arkle, by the way, was a famous race-horse.)

After Reading

● Many people have stories about going to the dentist – but what about looking at the situation from the other point of view? Working in pairs, write a list of questions which you could ask a dentist. Try to come up with questions which cannot be answered in one word; for example, rather than 'Do you treat lots of children?', ask 'How do you feel about treating children?' and 'Tell us about any particular children you remember treating.' Contact a local dentist and ask if you can interview him or her; say it will take about twenty minutes and make an appointment. Be on time for the appointment. Take a tape-recorder or make sure one of you can jot down good notes. Don't stick to your questions if something more interesting crops up – your aim is to get recollections and feelings, not bare facts. Your findings can then be written up into an article or recounted to a larger group. (Not everyone in a class will be able to interview a dentist, of course, unless there is an unusually high proportion of them living in your area. Your teacher will organize this and perhaps arrange for other pairs to interview other professions/trades/vocations.)

● We are all concerned with our appearance – but some people are more concerned than others! Why? When does an interest in your appearance become vanity? – or narcissism (look it up)?

● Imagine you are a visitor from another planet who has been observing the ways of humanoids in the UK sector of planet Earth. In this section of your report you are required to comment on the way the humanoids arrange the thin strands on the top of their craniums, the way they paint their facial areas and the way they drape their bodies with cloth and other materials. What differences do you detect between the two genders? What conclusions do you reach?

● Why do we have people whose full-time occupation is dealing with teeth and eyes but not with noses or ears or tongues or armpits? Write a story or a sketch which involves going to see the 'nasologist' for a check-up.

House-hunting

Before Reading

● What do you associate with the idea of 'house-hunting'? Is it usually a pleasant activity?

During Reading

● Look out for examples of the writer being torn between two opposite reactions to houses: seeing the faults on the one hand and wanting to overlook all the faults on the other.

After Reading

● Have you ever moved house? Write down your recollections in a fairly rough form, trying to remember as much as you can. Then, and only then, go and ask a grown up who was involved in the moving for their recollections. Are there any differences: (a) in facts, or (b) in feelings about the experience?

● Write a story based on the idea of either houses being physically moved from one place to another or house-hunting where the houses have to be hunted in the same way that foxes or deer are hunted.

● *'My word is my bond. Believe me, you have my word for it.'* Write a story or a scene from a play which features (amongst others if you wish) Mr Fox, a naive house-hunter and a suspicious friend of the house-hunter.

● Estate agents and car salesmen have a bad reputation. Do you think this is justified? Talk to at least one representative of each trade and to people who have had dealings with each trade. Write up your findings in an article with the title 'Martyrs or Con-men?', or something similar.

● Get some detailed house descriptions from an estate agent. Notice the way they are laid out and the sort of language used. Now write a description of a dog kennel/coal bunker/school cloakroom/sandcastle or somewhere equally unsuitable in a way which will persuade readers that it's a desirable home for a family.

● *'When my mother asked him if he was peckish, he wasn't at all sure whether he was or not.'* In a group, draw up a list of everyday expressions which a foreigner might have trouble with. Select the ten you think are the most important and write explanations which would be clear to someone speaking English as a second language. Compare the explanations in the group and select the ones which are most clear and precise, for example:

'Nip down the corner for a . . . ' might be explained as:
'Go to the shop at the end of the street for a . . . '

● Most of us have felt in two minds about something, as the writer does about the two houses which she likes, which nevertheless have lots of things wrong with them. Imagine yourself in a situation where you are looking at an item of clothing, a gift for someone, a record or a second-hand bicycle (for instance) and write a conversation between the two sides of your mind, for example:

A: Oh, it's great. What a terrific colour!
B: That colour never suits me.
A: That style is very fashionable.
B: It looks ridiculous on me and the style is on the way out.
A: Yes, but . . . (and so on)

At Longitude and Latitude

Before Reading

● What comes into your mind with the words 'Alone on a desert island'?

During Reading

● Pause after the third paragraph. What's going to happen? What sort of a person does the teller of the story seem to be? Do you assume the character is male or female? If you imagined a male, try reading these first few paragraphs through with a female character in mind. What difference does it make?

● Pause again after the sixth paragraph – has your idea of how the story will end changed?

After Reading

● This is a *short* short story – less than 1,000 words. It is probably similar in length to the pieces of writing you will have been doing. Do you find it too short? If so, what is missing?

● You may not find this story at all amusing. If you do, it will probably have something to do with the difference between the way you see the character and the way he sees himself. In which other stories or extracts in this book are there similar characters? Can you think of characters in radio or television comedies who are similarly unaware of how they appear to other people? This kind of innocence or naivety is most common in children, of course, and can be amusing, or touching, or nauseating. Do you know adults who are like this? Does it matter? Do we all have some of this inability to see ourselves as we really are? Perhaps the situation should be seen from the other way around: that other people fail to see us as we really are? Do people understand what you are really like?

> *I seem to be slow*
> *   But really I'm thinking*
> *I seem to be rude*
> *   But really I'm wondering what to say*
> *I seem to be forgetful*
> *   But really . . . .*

Write your own poem with the same *I seem to be . . . But really* plan as the one above. Aim for a minimum of ten lines. Be prepared to cross things out or move them around until it seems right to you.

● Write some of the conversation which is hinted at in the story, for example, on the dock as he sets off. This could also form the basis of a short piece of improvisation for a small group.

● Give the character a name and describe his preparations and the way he sets off from the point of view of one of the onlookers – perhaps Harold or Harold's wife.

● With a partner, discuss the following:
— What has happened to the island?
— Should we feel sorry for the storyteller?
— What would he do next?
Taking it in turns to write three of four lines at a time, continue the story.

● We, as readers, expect the character to reach the island and when he doesn't we may be shocked, annoyed, frustrated, amused . . . Write a short story which leads the reader to expect a certain sort of ending but conclude it in a totally different way.

● Write a script for 'Desert Island Discs' in which you are the celebrity.

Fiddler on the Roof

Before Reading

● What possible meanings could there be to the title?

During Reading

● Look out for the writer's reference to unexpected tools and implements – see if he actually recommends the use of any normal DIY tools.

After Reading

● Make an annotated diagram of one of the repair activities he describes, or draw a strip cartoon showing someone trying to carry out one or more of the repair jobs...

● Many people have DIY stories in the same way that they have stories about accidents and operations. Ask people you know to tell you about their experiences of house repairs or improvements, and then retell their stories in your own words.

● Heath Robinson was an artist who specialised in drawing ridiculously complicated contraptions. See what you can find out about him and try to find some examples of his work. When you've got an idea of the sort of machine or tool we now describe as 'heathrobinson' after the artist, draw a diagram of a machine for doing a task such as cleaning the gutters, getting cats out of trees, bringing in the washing without leaving the house, taking the dog for a walk, shaking the tomato ketchup bottle, or something of your own choosing.... Be prepared to describe the workings of the machine to a small group or to the class.

● How do you (or people you know) feel about heights? Think about trees, ladders, roofs, cliffs, mountains, castle towers and fairground rides such as the ferris wheel. Individually or in a small group, quickly jot down your thoughts. Work them into a short piece of writing – which might well be a poem. Possible titles and/or first lines could be *I hate heights*, or *I like to climb up high*, or *My dad's afraid of heights,* or *From up on top of....*

● Alan Coren's humour lies in treating something absurd in a serious manner. Here he uses the factual tone of voice of the DIY advice book or magazine. Using the same earnest tone of voice, and referring to plenty of helpful detail, write some advice to readers on something completely ridiculous, like how to attract members of the opposite sex by strapping pineapples (or other tropical fruit) to their knees, or passing oral exams by hypnotising the examiner.

Where else in this book can you find examples of the same kind of humour?

EXTENDED ASSIGNMENTS

1 Personal experience

● Many of the pieces of writing in this collection are based on the personal experiences of the writers. In which pieces is this most obvious? Which pieces are not based on personal experience? Are there some where you just cannot tell? A lot of writing comes from the writer's own experience, of course, but, as we can see from Spike Milligan's memoirs, for example, a lot can happen to that experience before it reaches its final form on paper.

Write a comparison of three or four of the prose pieces in this collection which are based on personal experience. Describe which you prefer and what you think goes towards making a good piece of autobiographical writing.

2 What makes people laugh?

● Sometimes humour comes from taking serious things (particularly danger) lightly, or the opposite – treating trivial things seriously. Where does this occur in the pieces you have read?

● Humour also comes from people saying or doing things of which they don't fully appreciate the full implications, for example, Little Tree or the character in 'At Longitude and Latitude'. Can you find other examples?

● Both of the above are, to some extent, examples of incongruity – the putting together of items which don't normally go together. (Puns, based on words or phrases having two possible meanings, are another example.) What other instances of this can you find in this collection? Is incongruity always funny?

● What else makes people laugh?

● Are there some subjects which are never appropriate for humour? Is it wrong to joke about religion – death – illness . . . ? If not, what does it depend on?

● Take a closer look at an example of television comedy and try to work out what it is that makes a programme funny. See if you can find examples of the types of humour mentioned above.

3 Time

● Some people claim that humour dates quickly. On the other hand, people still laugh at comedies written hundreds of years ago. What elements in humorous writing might become dated? What elements survive? How will the items in this collection fare, do you think? Are there some things in it which are more likely to stand the test of time than others?

4 Some of the items in this collection have serious messages under-lying their humour (honest!) See if you can find some examples of this.

5 Select three or four characters from different stories, poems or extracts in this book and write a sketch or a story which involves them all.

Poems: Follow On

GROUP A

'Daily Dilemmas'; 'The Diet';
'E322'; 'Giving Up Smoking'

Before Reading

● What do the words 'Food' and 'Health' conjure up in your mind?

During Reading

● What tone of voice is most appropriate for reading each of the poems? Would any of them be better read silently than aloud?

After Reading

● What are the reasons for going on a diet? Do some people diet unnecessarily? (See what Maria Morris has to say about appearance later on in this book.) Can you keep healthy without being a 'health fanatic'? Is overeating worse than smoking? Is alcohol worse than both? Gather your thoughts together and then, perhaps with a partner, and having done some research (talking to Home Economics/ Biology/PE teachers for a start), write an article for a magazine. A working title might be: 'Food, Drink, Exercise and Fags: a Guide for Non-fanatics!'

● Try out some dramatic readings of these and any other poems on similar topics.

● Continue this poem, based on 'The Twelve Days of Christmas':

On the first day of my diet
This is what I ate
A Low-cal Crispy Bread Snack.

On the second day of my diet
This is what I ate
Two tiny apples
And a Low-cal Crispy Bread Snack

On the third day of my diet
This is what I ate . . .

● Finish these three sentences:
—*I'm so hungry, I feel as though I'm* ...
—*I'm so thirsty, I feel as though I'm* ...
—*I'm so full, I feel as though I'm* ...
Working in groups of four or five, put your suggestions together to form three verses. The start of the first verse will be the same for all groups

> *I'm so hungry*
> *I feel as though I'm* ...

Now add your individual suggestions, for example:

> *... An empty bag in a vacuum cleaner*
> *A Trojan horse without the warriors*
> (etc)

The second verse will begin:

> *I'm so thirsty*
> *I feel as though I'm* ...

and so on.

● Write down five things you really like to eat. Describe each in detail but do not use more than one sentence, for example:
— *crisp grilled bacon with English mustard; crunchy corn flakes with the top of the milk* ...
In a group of four or five collect these descriptions together, perhaps choosing three from each person. Put them in the order you think best and add or remove words according to taste. Serve on a large sheet of paper, garnished with bold illustrations.

● Use the format of a recipe to write a description of something totally different. The last sentences of the previous activity may give you a guideline. Perhaps you could write a recipe for a party (*Take 25 assorted people between 14 and 18 and mix thoroughly in a large dimly lit room. Add a large helping of previously prepared music* ...), an exam, a school-day, a chemistry experiment, a game of hockey, and so on.

GROUP B

'Our Solar System'; 'Dead Thick'; 'An Essay Justifying the Place of Science in the School Curriculum'

Before Reading

● How much difference does the teacher make to a subject? How common is it to like the teacher but not the subject – and vice versa?

During Reading

● Look at the titles of the three poems in this section. What would you expect to follow each of them if you didn't know that they were poems?

After Reading

● The headteacher has seen the pupils milling about on the playing field in what seemed like a most disorderly fashion. You are the teacher who organized the model of the solar system. You are called to the head's office to explain yourself. Write the conversation which takes place.

● Alternatively, write a poem in the same style as Eric Finney's from the point of view of the teacher, describing what happened that afternoon.

● Carry out a survey of teachers on the subject of reading. Draw up a short questionnaire which might include the following questions:
—Is reading good for you?
—Why?
—What have you read in the last three months?
The findings from this survey could then be compared with the results you get from asking a different sample of adults.

● If pupils can represent the solar system, they could also represent the workings of other things, such as a bicycle, an electric bell, a car engine . . . How would you arrange it? Draw a diagram using pin-people and write a description in prose or poetry of what happened when it was tried. You will have to imagine the events for this last task, unless you can find a very understanding teacher to try out your ideas.

● Why are some subjects taught at school and others not? Why not First Aid, DIY or Self-Defence? Why doesn't everyone learn to type or to drive?
— Plan a timetable: (a) for 12 year old pupils, and (b) for 15 year old pupils, which you think would be ideal – not just for you but for the whole year group.
— In small groups, compare your timetables and decide on one (which might be a mixture of several original timetables) to put forward to the class.
— Each group should present its suggested timetable and be prepared to answer criticisms and questions from the other groups. An independent judge (perhaps from another class) could be asked to make a final decision on the best timetable.
— Perhaps a representative would like to present the suggestion to

the headteacher or deputy in charge of timetabling. His or her views could then be passed back to the class.

● Schools are not the most popular places. Pupils, teachers, parents (and members of the public who know nothing about them) all criticize them. How, then, could things be arranged better? What would be an acceptable and affordable way of organizing young people between the ages of 5 and 16? You could work on this in a similar way to the previous assignment, but it might be useful to get ideas from people outside the classroom before finalizing your own suggestions.

GROUP C

'nobody loses all the time'; 'The Grange'; 'Poor but Honest'; 'Exploding Heads'

Before Reading

● It used to be much more common for stories to be told in the form of poems. Why?

During Reading

● Pause after the first two verses of 'Poor but Honest' and 'nobody loses all the time' and suggest what will be recounted in the remainder of the poems.

After Reading

● Each of the poems in this section tells a story. Try composing a poem that tells a story.

● 'Poor but Honest' is a traditional song. Try writing some extra verses for it. You might begin one, 'He was rich, but he was wicked . . . ' It might turn into a whole song – poem on its own.

● What voices would be appropriate for reading the poems aloud? Prepare a reading of each of them, either individually or as a group.

● With a partner, work out what might have happened at 'The Grange'. Your description of events there should take account of all the hints in the poem, for example, about the butler, Miss Ursy, and so on. Write up your report with all relevant detail included – but aim to write a maximum of 500 words.

● Write an account of what happened in 'Exploding Heads' from the point of view of the Deputy or what happened in 'The Grange' from the point of view of the governess.

● In spite of the dire events related in the poems, none of them adopts a serious tone. What would be the effect of treating each of the stories related in the poems seriously? Could it be done successfully? Write a news story for the local paper based on 'Exploding Heads'.

● Here are some beginnings to possible story poems. Pick one and see how far you can continue it. You don't have to use these exact words, of course.

I have a cousin called
kev who is a born nuisance and
nearly everybody said he should have . . .

I have a mother called
mam who is a born worrier and . . .

Oh there hasn't been much change
At the Comp.
Of course the hole in the hedge is bigger . . .

Did I tell you about the day the Chemistry teacher
turned transparent?
  He was up on his stool
  At the start of the day
  About to pour H_2SO_4
  In the usual way . . .

S/he was the head, but s/he was human
  Victim of the government's whim
First they praised her/him, then they blamed her/him,
  And s/he lost . . .

S/he was young, but s/he was gorgeous/dozy/stubborn
  Victim of the deputy's tongue
– Its sarky comments, its sudden shouts –
  Till s/he didn't know right from wrong . . .

Further Reading

Alan Bleasdale is best known as a writer of plays, many of which have been televised, for example, *No More Sitting on the Old School Bench* and *The Boys from the Blackstuff*. If you enjoy his style and subject matter you may also like the plays of Willy Russell: *Breezeblock Park*, *Educating Rita* and *Our Day Out*. Another writer well known for his work for television is David Nobbs (*The Death of Reginald Perrin* and *The Return of Reginald Perrin*). His *Second To Last in the Sack Race* is very funny and has been a successful stage play.

Apart from his memoirs, Clive James has published several collections of weekly reviews of television programmes, for example *Glued to the Box*. Readers will already know about the other volumes of Spike Milligan's memoirs but may not be aware of his two novels, *The Looney* and *Puckoon*. Look out also for various versions of *The Goon Show Scripts* extracts from which would be ideal for recording. *Plays for Laughs* is worth mentioning here too – the collection by Johnny Ball, originally written for television.

Another writer with strong television connections is James Herriot. Many of his stories in the famous vet books are amusing. Try *A Vet in a Spin*, for instance. Writing in the same vein are Harry Cole and Robert Clifford, a policeman and doctor respectively. Their series of books, such as *Policeman's Progress* and *Surely Not, Doctor!*, record incidents, many of them funny, from their lengthy professional careers. Autobiography is also the source of humorous material in Caroline Akrill's series of books centred on the world of horse-riding, of which *Not Quite a Horse-Woman* is a good example.

If you enjoyed Sue Limb, look out for *Up the Garden Path*, and those who appreciated the spoof letters of Martha will enjoy *More from Martha* and Jill Tweedie's *It's Only Me*. Gwen Grant's *Lily Pickle Band Book* and *One Way Only* will be of interest to readers who liked the extract from *Private – Keep Out*.

J.P. Donleavy and Forrest Carter are writers for a more adult audience. In their very different ways they are both something of an acquired taste. At some stage you may like to try Donleavy's *Ginger Man* or *The Beastly Beattitudes of Balthazar B* – or Carter's *Outlaw Josey Wales* or *Watch for me on the Mountain*.

Though many younger readers enjoy him, Douglas Adams is also aiming at adult readership. His series of *Hitchhiker's Guide to the Galaxy* books are well known, the first two probably being the best. His most recent books are *Dirk Gently's Holistic Detective Agency* and its follow-up, *The Long Dark Tea Time of the Soul*.

Roald Dahl writes for adults and children. His books for children are full of humorous incidents and most can be enjoyed by readers of any age – *Danny the Champion of the World* and *Revolting Rhymes* for instance. He has written many short stories for adults, some of which have a certain macabre humour, for example *Someone Like You* and *Kiss Kiss*.

Helen Cresswell is best known as a writer for younger readers but her Bagthorpe series, starting with *Ordinary Jack* is much appreciated by adults too. Again, Norman Hunter and Richmal Crompton are seen as children's writers, but books such as Hunter's *Count Bakwerdz on the Carpet* and Crompton's *Just William* have a much wider appeal. (Anyone who has suffered from an irritating brother or sister will smile at the 'William the Intruder' in *Just William*.)

Finally, let me recommend two short stories from another volume in the Unwin Hyman Short Story Series, *Pigs is Pigs*. One is the title story by Ellis Parker Butler and the other is 'The Harry Hastings Method' by Warner Law.

Acknowledgements

Thanks for various kinds of help to Fiona Edwards, Irene Wallace, Claire Mellor, John Reeves, Keith Miller, Roy Blatchford and Ian McMillan.

The editor and publishers wish to thank the following for permission to reproduce copyright material:

'Bone Lines and 'E322 – or, Is My Mother Trying to Kill Me?', and 'Exploding Heads' © Trevor Millum 1989

January 1943 – At Sea © Spike Milligan, taken from *Adolf Hitler – My Part in His Downfall* reprinted by permission of Michael Joseph Ltd

Unreliable Memoirs © Clive James, reprinted by permission of Peters, Fraser and Dunlop Group Ltd

The Loaded Dog © Henry Lawson, taken from *Other Places Other Worlds* edited by Rhodri Jones, Heinemann Ltd

'Daily Dilemmas' © Natasha Josefowitz, taken from *Is This Where I Was Going?* published by Collumbus Books Ltd

'The Diet' © Maureen Burge, from *In The Pink*, published by The Women's Press

'Giving Up Smoking' © Wendy Cope, taken from *Making Cocoa for Kingsley Amis*, reproduced by permission of Faber & Faber

Goat's Tobacco © Roald Dahl, from *Boy*, published by Jonathan Cape and Penguin Books, reproduced by permission of Murray Pollinger Ltd

Where Did Our Pete Find this Tiger? © Gwen Grant taken from *Private – Keep Out* published by Armada

Snake in the Grass © Helen Cresswell, taken from *Mischief Makers*, edited by S Bowles, reproduced by permission of A M Heath & Co Ltd

A Night on the Mountain © Forrest Carter, taken from *The Edu-*

cation of Little tree by Forrest Carter, published by Macdonald & Co

'Our Solar System' © Eric Finney, first published in *Spaceways*, J Foster, (ed) published by OUP, 1986

'Dead Thick' © Brian Patten, from *Storm Damage*, Unwin Hyman 1989

'An Essay Justifying the Place of Science in the School Curriculum' © Jayne Hollinson, first published in IRON no. 53

Thoughts on Paper © Maria Morris, taken from *Bitter Sweet Dreams*, first published by Virago Press Ltd

Southward Bound © Alan Bleasdale, taken from *Scully* by Alan Bleasdale, reproduced by permission of Harvey Unna and Stephen Durbridge Ltd

Abscess Makes the Heart Grow Fonder © Maureen Lipman, taken from *How Was it for You'?* published by Robson Books Ltd

'nobody loses all the time' © ee cummings, from *Complete Poems*, published by Grafton Books (a division of William Collins & Sons)

'The Grange' © Stevie Smith, taken from *The Collected Poems of Stevie Smith* (Penguin Modern Classics) reproduced by permission of James MacGibbon, executor

House Hunting © Sue Limb, 1987, taken from *Love Forty* published by Corgi

At Longitude and Latitude © JP Donleavy, taken from *Meet My Maker the Mad Molecule*, published by The Bodley Head

Dear Mary © Jill Tweedie, taken from *Letters from a Fainthearted Feminist*, reproduced by permission of Robson Books Ltd

'Please Keep Off the Grass' © Peter Tinsley, taken from *Poems by Children* edited by M Baldwin, published by Routledge

Fiddler on the Roof © Alan Coren, taken from *Bin Ends*, published by Sphere, 1988

While the publishers have made every effort to trace and contact copyright holders, we would be pleased to hear from anyone not correctly acknowledged.